Timeless Amigurumi Doll Pattern

Crochet Doll Patterns for All Skill Levels

By SONIA KENZIE

Table of Contents

Introduction

Welcome to the Magical World of Amigurumi!

A certain magic comes to life when a skein of yarn meets a crochet hook. It's a magic that transforms a simple strand into something tangible, bringing joy and comfort. It's magic that weaves stories and creates companions, and it's magic that has captured my heart for as long as I can remember.

In the following pages, I invite you to embark on a journey with me into the enchanting world of amigurumi. Derived from the Japanese words "ami" (meaning crocheted or knitted) and "nuigurumi" (meaning stuffed doll), amigurumi represents a craft that marries creativity with technique, resulting in the creation of utterly charming dolls.

What makes amigurumi truly special is its remarkable versatility. Whether you're a seasoned crocheter with a treasure trove of yarn or a newcomer to the craft, this book is designed to be your trusted companion. The patterns within these pages cater to all skill levels, ensuring that you'll find a project that speaks to you no matter where you are in your crochet journey.

For those new to the world of crochet, fear not! The initial chapters will gently guide you through the essentials, from understanding basic stitches to deciphering the language of crochet patterns. And for the experienced crocheter, rest assured that the patterns presented here are crafted with an eye for detail and a love for the craft I'm eager to share with you.

With every stitch, you'll create a doll and a little piece of magic. These amigurumi dolls have a unique ability to bring smiles, evoke nostalgia, and ignite the spark of creativity. Whether they find a home on a shelf, in a child's arms, or become a cherished gift for a loved one, each doll carries the love and care you've poured into its creation.

So, dear reader, let's embark on this crochet adventure together.

Let's explore the wonderful world of amigurumi and let our hooks and yarn bring to life a cast of characters that will warm hearts and spark imaginations. It's time to pick up your crochet hook and let the magic begin!

Chapter 1: Getting Started with Amigurumi

1.1 The Tools of the Trade

Essential Gear: Your Crochet Arsenal

Before diving into the stitches and patterns that will bring your amigurumi dolls to life, let's familiarize ourselves with the essential tools every crocheter needs.

- *Choosing the Right Crochet Hook*: your crochet hook is an extension of your creativity. Explore the sizes and materials available and find the one that feels comfortable in your hands. A smaller hook is often preferred for amigurumi to create tight stitches and achieve a firm structure.

- *Anatomy of a Crochet Hook*: understanding the anatomy of a crochet hook is like knowing the parts of a musical instrument. Each component is crucial in how the hook feels in your hands and influences your stitching.
  Head: The rounded tip that catches the yarn.
  Throat: The groove beneath the head that holds the yarn.
  Shaft: The body of the hook, determining stitch size.
  Handle: The grip area provides comfort during extended use.

- *The Harmony of Hook Sizes*: crochet hooks come in various sizes, and each size produces stitches of different dimensions. The sizing convention may vary between countries, but the principle remains consistent—smaller hooks create tighter stitches, while larger hooks yield looser stitches. Familiarize yourself with the standardized metric and US letter sizing to choose the right hook for your project confidently.

- *Material Matters*: crochet hooks are crafted from various materials, including aluminum, steel, wood, and plastic. Each material offers a unique feel and weight, influencing your stitching speed and comfort. Explore different materials to discover which resonates best with your crocheting style.

- *Selecting the Perfect Yarn*: yarn is the soul of amigurumi. Its texture, weight, and color contribute to the personality of your creation. From the soft embrace of cotton to the plush coziness of acrylic, each yarn type brings a unique character to your dolls. Consider the preferences of your doll, the desired size, and the level of huggability you want to achieve.

- *Additional Tools for Precision*: While a crochet hook and yarn are the leading players, a few additional tools can enhance your amigurumi experience. Stitch markers, embroidery needles, and stuffing materials are among the essentials. We'll delve into their roles as we progress in our amigurumi adventure.

1.2 Understanding Yarn Weight and Fiber

Not all yarns are created equal, and understanding the intricacies of yarn weight and fiber is crucial to creating the perfect amigurumi doll. Yarn weight determines the yarn's thickness and directly influences your doll's size and appearance. From lace weight to super bulky, each category has its unique characteristics. Discover the art of balancing yarn weight with project requirements to achieve the desired result.

Fiber choice adds a layer of creativity to your amigurumi. Cotton yarns provide a smooth finish, while wool adds warmth and texture. Acrylic yarns are vibrant and easy to care for. Consider the qualities you want your doll to possess, and let the yarn guide you in creating a masterpiece.

Stitch markers are the navigational aids in your crochet journey, signaling transitions, increases, and decreases. Explore the variety of stitch markers, from simple rings to whimsical shapes, and understand how they enhance the precision of your amigurumi.

Embroidery needles are the sculptors of your creation, allowing you to add intricate details and expressions to your dolls. Learn about the different needle types and sizes, each serving a specific purpose in embellishment.

The stuffing inside your amigurumi is more than mere fluff—it gives shape and character to your dolls. Delve into stuffing materials, from traditional polyfill to eco-friendly alternatives, and master the art of achieving the perfect level of plumpness. For a polished finish, blocking tools come into play. Explore blocking mats, pins, and steamers, and discover how they contribute to refining the shape and appearance of your amigurumi.

Safety eyes and noses add a touch of realism to your dolls. Delve into the world of these secure embellishments, understanding how to attach them safely and precisely to bring your amigurumi's face to life. As you familiarize yourself with these additional tools, consider them the accompaniment to your crochet hook's melody, working together to compose a harmonious amigurumi symphony.

1.3 Mastering Basic Stitches

The Foundation: Crochet Stitches for Amigurumi

Now that we're acquainted with our tools and yarn, it's time to dive into the foundation of crochet—the stitches.

- **Single Crochet: The Versatile Stitch:** The single crochet stitch is the cornerstone of amigurumi. It creates a tight, dense fabric ideal for stuffing. Learn the proper technique, practice tension control, and master the single crochet as it forms the basis for most amigurumi patterns.

- **Double Crochet and Beyond:** While the single crochet is fundamental, the double crochet and half-double crochet stitches expand your repertoire. These stitches add variety, allowing you to create unique textures and shapes in your dolls. We'll guide you through each stitch, ensuring a solid foundation for your amigurumi journey.

1.4 Reading Patterns and Abbreviations

Crochet patterns are their own language, and decoding this language is a crucial skill for any amigurumi enthusiast. In this section, we'll unravel the mystery behind crochet abbreviations. From "sc" for single crochet to "inc" for increase, understanding these shorthand notations is vital to following patterns seamlessly. I aim to empower you to pick up any amigurumi pattern and bring it to life.

Crochet patterns are a rich tapestry of abbreviations and symbols, creating a language that, at first glance, might seem cryptic. However, you'll make stunning amigurumi fluently once you decipher this poetic code. Let's delve into the ABCs (or SCs, HDCs, and DCs?) of crochet abbreviations.

The Stitching Alphabet:

Ch: Chain

How to Read: "Ch 5" means you create a chain of five stitches.

Purpose: The foundation of many crochet projects, creating chains, is akin to casting on in knitting.

SC: Single Crochet

How to Read: "SC 10" signifies working ten single crochet stitches.

Purpose: A fundamental yet versatile stitch, creating a dense and sturdy fabric.

HDC: Half Double Crochet

How to Read: "HDC 8" instructs you to half double crochet eight stitches.

Purpose: Slightly taller than a single crochet, balancing height and density.

DC: Double Crochet

How to Read: "DC 12" directs you to double-crochet twelve stitches.

Purpose: A classic stitch, forming a looser and more open fabric than single or half double crochet.

TR: Treble Crochet

How to Read: "TR 15" tells you to treble crochet fifteen stitches.

Purpose: A tall stitch, perfect for creating airy and lightweight projects.

Combining Stitches:

SC2TOG: Single Crochet Two Together

How to Read: "SC2TOG" means to decrease by single crocheting two stitches together.

Purpose: Creates a decrease, helpful in shaping your amigurumi.

INC: Increase

How to Read: "INC" indicates an increase, often by working two stitches into one.

Purpose: Adds stitches to create a more comprehensive piece.

Directions and Techniques:

FO: Fasten Off

How to Read: "FO" instructs you to finish your work, securing the last stitch.

Purpose: Essential for completing a project and neatly fastening the yarn.

BLO: Back Loop Only

How to Read: "SC BLO" only directs you to a single crochet in the back loop.

Purpose: Alters the texture of the fabric, creating ridges or patterns.

SL ST: Slip Stitch

How to Read: "SL ST to the first stitch" means to slip stitch to join.

Purpose: Used for joining rounds, creating a seamless appearance.

REP: Repeat

How to Read: "REP Rows 3-6" signifies repeating the specified rows.

Purpose: Saves space in patterns and streamlines instructions.

The Symbolic Language

Beyond abbreviations, crochet patterns often use symbols to convey actions. While variations exist, common symbols include "X" for a chain, "+" for a single crochet, and "T" for a treble crochet. These symbols provide an additional layer of clarity, especially for visual learners. As you embark on your amigurumi adventure, consider these abbreviations as the poetic verses that guide you through the rhythmic dance of stitches, transforming a strand of yarn into a masterpiece.

1.5 Starting Your First Project

It's time to put theory into practice. Armed with the knowledge of tools, yarn, stitches, and pattern interpretation, we'll embark on your first amigurumi project. Selecting the correct pattern for your skill level is crucial; I recommend beginner-friendly patterns, ensuring your first amigurumi experience is enjoyable and rewarding. Follow our step-by-step instructions as we create your chosen doll together. From the initial magic ring to the finishing touches, we'll be by your side, offering tips and encouragement. Remember, every stitch is a step closer to bringing your amigurumi creation to life, embrace the journey with an open heart and a sense of adventure. Every stitch celebrates your creativity, and every doll is a testament to your unique expression. Let the yarn guide your hands and imagination, and may your amigurumi adventure be filled with joy, discovery, and endless possibilities.

Chapter 2: Types of Crochet

2.1 Traditional Crochet

Traditional crochet is the cornerstone of this diverse craft, weaving a rich tapestry of stitches that have endured through generations. In this section, we'll delve deeper into the artistry of traditional crochet, uncovering its history, mastering foundational stitches, and exploring its boundless versatility.

Traditional crochet has a storied past, dating back centuries and evolving across cultures. From delicate lace doilies to robust afghans, the enduring appeal of conventional crochet lies in its ability to adapt to various styles and purposes. We'll journey through time, tracing the roots of traditional crochet and understanding how it has shaped the broader crochet landscape.

At the heart of traditional crochet are foundational stitches, each with unique charm. In this exploration, we'll revisit the basics and delve into the nuances of stitches like the half-double crochet, treble crochet, and more. Understanding the anatomy of each stitch is critical to unlocking their creative potential.

* **The Single Crochet: A Sturdy Foundation.** The single crochet stitch is the building block of many projects, providing a sturdy and tight foundation. We'll explore its versatility in amigurumi, where precision and structure are paramount.
* **The Double Crochet: Balancing Speed and Height.** Move beyond the single crochet to the double crochet, a stitch that adds height to your work without compromising speed. Discover how this stitch contributes to the intricate details of amigurumi dolls.
* **The Half-Double Crochet: A Midway Marvel.** The half-double crochet between the single and double crochet offers a balance of height and tightness. Dive into its applications, especially in creating textures for amigurumi.
* **The Treble Crochet: Reaching New Heights.** For projects that demand height, the treble crochet is indispensable. Uncover its role in crafting larger amigurumi dolls and adding a touch of elegance to your creations.

Beyond the Basics: Textures and Techniques.

Traditional crochet extends far beyond the fundamental stitches. As we venture into textures and techniques, you'll discover how to incorporate post and shell stitches into your amigurumi projects.

* **Front and Back Post Stitches: Sculpting Surfaces.** Master the art of front and back post stitches, elevating your amigurumi with sculpted surfaces. These techniques are precious in creating defined features like facial expressions and clothing textures.

* **Shell Stitches: Crafting Elegance.** Explore the elegance of shell stitches, a cluster of stitches that mimics the shape of a shell. Uncover how this technique adds a decorative flourish to your amigurumi dolls, enhancing their visual appeal.

Crafting with Color: Intarsia and Fair Isle Techniques

Traditional crochet offers a canvas for color exploration, and in this segment, we'll delve into techniques like intarsia and Fair Isle. These methods enable you to introduce intricate color patterns to your amigurumi, transforming them into vibrant and captivating creations.

* **Intarsia: Painting with Yarn.** Master the art of intarsia, a technique that allows you to create blocks of color within your crochet work. Discover how this method opens doors to designing amigurumi with intricate color details, making each doll a unique masterpiece.

* **Fair Isle Crochet: Harmonizing Colors.** Inspired by the knitting tradition, Fair Isle Crochet introduces colorwork through stranded techniques. We'll guide you through harmonizing colors in your amigurumi dolls, creating eye-catching patterns that evoke warmth and charm.

Versatility in Every Stitch: Applications in Amigurumi

As we conclude our exploration of traditional crochet, we'll showcase its versatile applications in amigurumi. When harnessed with creativity, traditional stitches, and techniques breathe life into your dolls, giving them character and individuality.

* **Sculpting Details: Faces, Hair, and Clothing.** Use traditional crochet stitches to sculpt intricate details in your amigurumi dolls. From shaping facial features to crafting hair with textured stitches, classic crochet becomes a powerful tool for personalizing your creations.

* **Seamless Joints and Limbs.** Achieve seamless joints and limbs through traditional crochet techniques. Discover the art of attaching body parts, creating movable joints, and ensuring your amigurumi dolls are adorable and structurally sound.

* **Designing Clothing and Accessories.** Traditional crochet opens a world of

possibilities when dressing your amigurumi dolls. Whether it's crafting miniature outfits, intricate accessories, or even tiny shoes, traditional stitches provide the foundation for an expansive wardrobe.

In unraveling the layers of traditional crochet, we find not just a craft but a living tradition that continues to evolve. It's a testament to the enduring appeal and boundless creativity that traditional crochet brings to the enchanting world of amigurumi. As you embark on your amigurumi adventure, let the stitches of tradition be your guide, shaping each doll with precision, passion, and a touch of timeless elegance.

2.2 Tunisian Crochet

Tunisian crochet is a captivating fusion of crochet and knitting techniques; it has a rich history, with roots stretching back to the craft's earliest days. Originally known as the "Afghan Stitch," it gained popularity in the mid-19th century. Delve into the historical tapestry of Tunisian crochet, understanding its evolution and the cultural influences that have shaped its development. In this section, we'll unravel the unique beauty of Tunisian crochet, exploring its distinct stitches, discussing its historical roots, and showcasing how it can elevate your amigurumi creations.

At the heart of Tunisian crochet lies a tapestry of stitches that create a fabric distinct from traditional crochet. The Tunisian simple stitch, Tunisian knit stitch, and Tunisian purl stitch are just a few threads in this rich tapestry. Explore the Tunisian simple stitch, the cornerstone of Tunisian crochet. Uncover its tight, woven texture and understand how it provides the perfect foundation for amigurumi dolls, giving them a neat and polished appearance.

Dive into the Tunisian knit stitch, a technique that mimics the look of knitted fabric. Discover how this stitch adds depth and texture to your amigurumi, creating a unique visual appeal that sets your dolls apart. Master the Tunisian purl stitch, which introduces a textured, bumpy surface. Learn how this stitch can create patterns and designs, making your amigurumi dolls stand out with intricate detailing. Tunisian crochet introduces a new dimension to amigurumi, allowing crocheters to explore textures and patterns not easily achievable with traditional stitches. We'll guide you through the applications of Tunisian crochet in crafting amigurumi dolls, from creating unique textures on the doll's body to fashioning clothing and accessories.

Experiment with Tunisian crochet to craft textured body elements for your amigurumi dolls.

Whether adding a ribbed pattern to arms or creating a bumpy texture for a whimsical creature, Tunisian crochet opens doors to endless possibilities. Explore how Tunisian crochet can be harnessed to design intricate patterns for amigurumi clothing. From miniature sweaters with cable-like details to blankets draped over your dolls, Tunisian stitches bring sophistication to your creations. Master the art of seamless joining and shaping with Tunisian crochet. Create dolls with smooth, continuous surfaces and experiment with shaping techniques that enhance the overall aesthetic of your amigurumi.

Exploring Colorwork with Tunisian Crochet

Tunisian crochet provides a canvas for stunning colorwork, and in this segment, we'll guide you through techniques like entrelac and color changes. Learn how to introduce vibrant hues and intricate patterns to your amigurumi dolls, turning them into art.

Delve into the mesmerizing world of entrelac, a technique that creates a woven appearance by interlocking squares. Uncover how this method can be applied to amigurumi, adding a visual depth that captivates the eye. Master seamless color changes in Tunisian crochet, ensuring that your amigurumi dolls boast a polished and professional finish. Whether it's transitioning between colors for a multicolored body or adding accents, we'll guide you through the steps.

The Allure of Tunisian Crochet: Tips and Tricks

As we conclude our exploration of Tunisian crochet, we'll provide invaluable tips and tricks to enhance your proficiency. From selecting the right Tunisian crochet hook to maintaining tension and troubleshooting common issues, this section empowers you to incorporate Tunisian crochet into your amigurumi projects confidently.

Tunisian crochet opens the door to elegance and intricacy in the realm of amigurumi. As you embark on this creative journey, let the interplay of Tunisian stitches and traditional crochet techniques be your guide, shaping dolls that capture the heart and showcase the beauty of a craft that seamlessly blends history, artistry, and contemporary creativity.

2.3 Filet Crochet

Filet crochet is an enchanting technique that allows crocheters to create delicate, lacy designs within a grid-like structure. This section delves into the intricacies of filet crochet, explores its history, understands the fundamental stitches, and unveils how it can add an exquisite touch to your amigurumi creations. It has a storied history, dating back to the late 19th century.

Originating in Europe, particularly France and Italy, it gained popularity as a means of crafting decorative lace pieces. Dive into the tapestry of filet crochet, tracing its evolution from intricate tablecloths to contemporary applications in amigurumi.

The Grid: Foundation of Filet Crochet

At the heart of filet crochet lies the grid—a structured framework that serves as the canvas for your artistic expressions. We'll guide you through the basics of creating and understanding the grid, empowering you to design intricate patterns that elevate your amigurumi dolls. Explore the two fundamental elements of the filet crochet grid: mesh openings and solid blocks. Understand how the arrangement of these elements forms the basis of your design, allowing you to craft patterns that range from simple and elegant to complex and ornate. Deciphering filet crochet charts is a valuable skill. We'll provide a step-by-step guide on interpreting charts demystifying the symbols and stitches used. By the end, you'll be equipped to tackle any filet crochet pattern with confidence.

Filet Stitches: Building Lacework

In this segment, we'll unravel the stitches that create the enchanting lacework characteristic of filet crochet. From the foundational chain and double crochet to more advanced techniques like lace stitches, you'll gain insights into how each stitch contributes to the overall design. Master the art of creating the chain and double crochet stitches—the building blocks of filet crochet. Understand their role in forming the mesh and solid elements, setting the stage for intricate patterns. Elevate your filet crochet creations with lace stitches. Learn how to create openings within the solid blocks, adding dimension and intricacy to your lacework. These stitches open up possibilities for crafting unique textures in amigurumi clothing, accessories, and more.

Designing with Filet Crochet in Amigurumi

Filet crochet seamlessly integrates into amigurumi, offering a delicate touch to your dolls. Explore how to incorporate filet crochet into different elements of your amigurumi creations, from clothing to decorative accents. Enhance the elegance of your amigurumi doll's clothing with delicate lace edgings crafted through filet crochet. We'll guide you through adding lace trims to hems, sleeves, and collars, transforming your doll's wardrobe into a showcase of intricate craftsmanship. Discover how filet crochet can create personalized accents for your amigurumi dolls. From monograms to intricate motifs, filet crochet provides a unique avenue for customization, allowing you to infuse your creations with character and charm.

Troubleshooting and Tips for Filet Crochet Mastery

As you embark on your filet crochet journey, we'll provide insights into common challenges and share expert tips for mastering this technique. This section aims to ensure a smooth and enjoyable filet crochet experience, from maintaining tension to troubleshooting errors.

Filet crochet adds an exquisite layer of artistry to the world of amigurumi. As you experiment with creating delicate lace patterns and incorporating filet crochet into your dolls, let the mesh of stitches be a canvas for your creativity. Unveil the allure of filet crochet and watch as your amigurumi creations come to life with an added touch of timeless elegance.

2.4 Freeform Crochet

Freeform crochet is a liberating and expressive form of craft that encourages crocheters to break free from traditional patterns and rules. In this section, we'll explore the boundless world of freeform crochet, from its origins to guiding you through letting your creativity run wild.

Freeform crochet, often likened to painting with yarn, emerged as a countercultural movement in the mid-20th century. Artists sought a form of expression that transcended the structure of traditional crochet. Delve into the history of freeform crochet, tracing its roots in the art world and understanding how it has evolved into a beloved practice among crocheters. At its core, freeform crochet is about breaking boundaries and embracing imperfections. We'll delve into the philosophy of freeform, where there are no strict rules, and creativity knows no limits. Learn to appreciate the beauty in irregular shapes, varied stitches, and the unique character that emerges when you let your intuition guide the crochet hook.

Getting Started with Freeform Crochet

Embarking on a freeform crochet project can be both exciting and intimidating. We'll guide you through the initial steps, from selecting a diverse range of yarn to choosing a color palette that resonates with your artistic vision. Understand how to create a foundation for your freeform piece, setting the stage for exploring textures and shapes.

Discover the importance of yarn selection in freeform crochet. Explore a variety of textures, weights, and colors to add depth and contrast to your work. From plush wools to shimmering threads, each yarn choice contributes to the overall aesthetic of your freeform creation.

Unlike traditional crochet, freeform projects often begin without a clear pattern. Learn how to create a foundation chain that serves as the starting point for your freeform masterpiece. This initial chain provides a framework for building layers of stitches and embellishments.

Techniques in Freeform Crochet

Freeform crochet allows for the integration of various stitches and techniques. We'll explore how to incorporate unique stitches, experiment with different stitch heights, and seamlessly transition between motifs. Gain insights into the art of shaping and sculpting your freeform piece as it evolves organically. Dive into the world of stitch variations in freeform crochet. From basic single crochet to intricate popcorn stitches, we'll showcase how experimenting with different stitches adds texture and visual interest to your work. Unleash your creativity by combining stitches in unexpected ways.

Freeform crochet embraces the organic flow of shapes and contours. Learn techniques for shaping your project without the constraints of traditional patterns. Whether creating undulating waves or sculpting three-dimensional elements, freeform allows you to explore the sculptural potential of crochet.

Embracing Imperfections: Troubleshooting in Freeform Crochet

We'll address common challenges and offer troubleshooting tips as you navigate the freeform crochet process. Understand how to embrace imperfections as part of the artistic journey and learn techniques for incorporating unexpected elements into your creation.

Personalizing Amigurumi with Freeform Elements

Freeform crochet isn't limited to large projects—it can also enhance your amigurumi creations. Discover how to infuse your dolls with freeform elements, from incorporating textured patches to creating unique accessories. Unleash your imagination and let freeform crochet become a signature feature in your amigurumi designs.

The Joy of Freeform Crochet

In the realm of freeform crochet, the joy lies in the creation process. Whether you're a seasoned crocheter or a beginner, embrace the freedom of exploring shapes, textures, and colors without constraints. Allow the spontaneity of freeform crochet to infuse your amigurumi dolls with a touch of artistic expression that makes each creation one-of-a-kind.

2.5 Broomstick Lace Crochet

Broomstick lace crochet is a captivating technique that adds an elegant touch to your crochet repertoire. In this section, we'll dive deeper into broomstick lace, exploring its history and unique mechanics and guiding you through the steps to create exquisite lacework.

Broomstick lace crochet, or "jiffy lace" or "peacock eye crochet," has a rich history in function and fashion. Explore the origins of this technique, from its helpful use in creating warm fabrics to its evolution into a delicate and intricate lacework craft. Discover how broomstick lace has stood the test of time, captivating crocheters with its timeless beauty. At the heart of broomstick lace crochet is the creation of elongated loops, imparting a lacy and openwork effect to the fabric. We'll break down the fundamental mechanics of broomstick lace, from selecting the right "broomstick" (or dowel) to understanding the role of the crochet hook. Gain insights into the unique combination of stitches that form the foundation of broomstick lace. You'll need specific materials that complement the technique to embark on your broomstick lace crochet journey. Explore the ideal yarn choices, from lightweight cotton for a delicate touch to bulkier yarns that showcase the boldness of broomstick lace. Additionally, we'll guide you in selecting the suitable dowel or broomstick, ensuring a seamless and enjoyable crocheting experience.

   ☐ **Choosing the Right Yarn: Texture and Weight**

The suitable yarn can elevate your broomstick lace project. Delve into the considerations for choosing yarn texture and weight to achieve the desired drape and visual impact. Whether you're aiming for a breezy summer shawl or an intricate afghan, we'll guide you in making informed yarn selections.

   ☐ **Selecting a Dowel or Broomstick**

While a traditional broomstick was once used for this technique, today's crocheters have various options for creating loops. Explore different dowel materials and sizes, crochet hooks with additional features, and even purpose-built tools for broomstick lace. Understand how these choices impact the size and appearance of your lacework.

Broomstick lace crochet involves a set of stitches that come together to form its signature loops. We'll guide you through creating a bare broomstick lace strip, from the foundation chain to the final loop bind-off. Learn the rhythm of the stitches and develop the confidence to incorporate broomstick lace into various projects.

☐ Foundation Chain and First Loops

Begin your broomstick lace adventure by creating a foundation chain and initiating the first loops. Understand the role of the crochet hook in forming loops over the dowel, making the distinctive appearance of broomstick lace. Follow a step-by-step walkthrough to ensure a smooth start to your lacework.

☐ Building Height: Additional Rows

As your broomstick lace project progresses, we'll explore how to add height by working additional rows. Learn the sequence of stitches that build upon the initial loops, creating a beautifully textured fabric. Discover the versatility of broomstick lace in designing scarves, wraps, and even sections of larger projects.

Once you've mastered the foundational broomstick lace techniques, it's time to explore variations that add complexity and visual interest to your projects. From incorporating color changes to experimenting with stitch combinations, we'll introduce you to advanced broomstick lace concepts that elevate your crochet skills.

☐ Introducing Color: Stripes and Blends

Explore the creative possibilities of introducing color to your broomstick lace projects. Whether you prefer bold stripes or subtle blends, we'll guide you through techniques for seamless color transitions. Learn how to strategically place colors to enhance your lacework's texture and visual appeal.

☐ Stitch Combinations: Texture and Intricacy

Take your broomstick lace to the next level by experimenting with stitch combinations. Combine classic broomstick lace stitches with crochet techniques to create intricate textures and patterns. Gain inspiration for incorporating these advanced elements into shawls, blankets, and decorative items. To inspire your broomstick lace creativity, we'll showcase various projects that highlight this technique's versatility. Discover how broomstick lace can be applied to different items in your crochet repertoire, from elegant shawls to statement-making accessories. Explore patterns and ideas that cater to various skill levels.

☐ Elegant Shawl: Draping in Lace

Unlock the secrets to creating an elegant broomstick lace shawl that drapes gracefully over the shoulders. Follow a detailed pattern combining basic and advanced techniques, resulting in a sophisticated accessory suitable for casual and formal occasions.

   □ **Statement-Making Scarf: A Quick and Stylish Project**

For those looking for a quicker project with a bold impact, we'll guide you through crafting a statement-making broomstick lace scarf. Explore stitch variations and embellishments that turn a simple accessory into a fashionable statement piece. As you delve into broomstick lace crochet, we'll address common challenges and offer valuable tips for a seamless crocheting experience. From maintaining even tension to troubleshooting mistakes, this section will empower you to tackle any hurdles and enhance your mastery of broomstick lace. Broomstick lace crochet invites you into timeless elegance and intricate design. Whether you're a beginner or an experienced crocheter, embrace the opportunity to infuse your projects with the grace of broomstick lace. From delicate accessories to oversized garments, let this section be your guide to mastering the art of creating lace with a broomstick and crochet hook.

2.6 Exploring Hybrid Techniques

The crochet world is constantly evolving, and this section invites you to explore the exciting realm of hybrid techniques. By blending various crochet methods, you can push the boundaries of traditional crochet and create genuinely unique amigurumi dolls.

Discover the art of combining stitches from different crochet techniques. Whether integrating Tunisian stitches into traditional crochet or incorporating filet crochet elements, we'll guide you through seamlessly blending techniques.

Explore how combining different crochet styles can result in stunning and eclectic amigurumi. From combining freeform elements with structured stitches to marrying the elegance of broomstick lace with the simplicity of traditional crochet, this section sparks your creativity.

As you experiment with hybrid techniques, you'll naturally gravitate towards a style that feels uniquely yours. This section encourages you to embrace this journey of self-discovery, helping you define your signature crochet style that sets your amigurumi dolls apart. In the diverse landscape of crochet, each technique is a brushstroke on the canvas of creativity. As we explore these varied crochet styles, remember that there are no strict rules—only opportunities to experiment, create, and infuse your amigurumi dolls with a touch of your unique artistic expression.

Chapter 3: Language of Crochet

Crocheting, much like any language, has its own set of nuances and intricacies. In this chapter, we embark on a journey to decipher the language of crochet, unlocking the secrets that transform a simple skein of yarn into a masterpiece. The language of crochet, conveyed through patterns, abbreviations, and special techniques, is a vibrant tapestry waiting to be woven by your skilled hands.

3.1 Decoding Crochet Patterns

Crochet patterns are the blueprints that guide you through the intricate process of creating beautiful amigurumi dolls. In this section, we delve deeper into the art of decoding crochet patterns, demystifying the components, and providing you with the keys to unlock the full potential of your creative journey.

Title: Beyond a simple name, the title sets the tone for your project; it hints at the theme or style of the amigurumi doll you're about to bring to life. Pay attention to descriptive words that offer insights into the final creation—whether it's a whimsical creature, a regal character, or a charming animal.

Materials List: A well-prepared crocheter is a confident crocheter. The materials list is your shopping list for the creative journey. It provides a detailed inventory of everything you need, from the specific yarn colors and quantities to the type and size of the crochet hook. Take the time to gather all your materials before starting, ensuring a smooth and uninterrupted crafting experience.

Introduction: Often overlooked, the introduction sets the mood for the pattern. It may include the designer's inspiration, a brief story about the amigurumi, or even tips for customization. Read the introduction—it's the prelude to your creative adventure.

Body: The heart of the pattern lies in the step-by-step instructions. Each line is a carefully crafted directive that, when followed, transforms simple stitches into a three-dimensional masterpiece. As you read, visualize each step and how it contributes to the overall form of your amigurumi. Remember, patience is the key; take one step at a time.

Finishing and Assembly: The last leg of the pattern journey, this section guides you through the final touches and assembly of your amigurumi. It's the stage where individual pieces form the complete doll. Pay attention to specific instructions for stuffing, attaching limbs, or adding final details.

Images and Diagrams: A picture is worth a thousand words, and in crochet patterns, images and diagrams are crucial in conveying complex steps. Take advantage of these visual aids to ensure you're on the right path. Look for close-up shots of specific stitches, assembly diagrams, and any visual cues accompanying written instructions.

Charts: Some patterns include charts, visually representing the stitches and their placement. While charts might seem daunting initially, they can be invaluable, especially for complex stitch patterns or intricate designs. Please familiarize yourself with the symbols used in the chart and practice interpreting them alongside written instructions.

Tips for Deciphering Patterns:

1. **Read Carefully:** Before picking up your crochet hook, read the entire pattern thoroughly. Understanding the full scope of the project prevents surprises and helps you prepare mentally for each step.

2. **Mark Your Progress:** Use stitch markers, highlighters, or a simple pencil to mark off completed rows or sections, keep you organized, and provide a visual sense of accomplishment.

3. **Clarify Ambiguities:** Crochet patterns, like any form of communication, can have ambiguities. If a particular step seems unclear, seek clarification from online crochet communities, forums, or directly from the pattern designer. Don't hesitate to ask questions—the crochet community is welcoming and supportive.

4. **Take Breaks:** Crocheting is a joyful but intricate process. If you encounter frustration or confusion, take short breaks. Sometimes, stepping away and returning with fresh eyes can make a challenging pattern more manageable.

Remember, a crochet pattern is your companion on the creative journey. As you decode the language of crochet patterns, you'll not only master the technical aspects but also develop an intuitive understanding of how stitches come together to form delightful amigurumi creations.

3.2 Crochet Abbreviations and Terms

Crochet, like any language, has its abbreviations and terms. In this section, we'll delve into the crochet lexicon, breaking down commonly used abbreviations and terms to ensure you can confidently decipher any crochet pattern that comes your way.

Chain Stitch (CH):

The foundation of many crochet projects, the chain stitch is abbreviated as CH. It creates a base chain that serves as the starting point for your work. Mastering the chain stitch is fundamental, setting the stage for subsequent rows and rounds.

How to Chain:

1. Make a slipknot.
2. Insert the hook into the slipknot.
3. Yarn over and pull through the slipknot.
4. Repeat steps 2-3 to create a chain of desired length.

Single Crochet (SC):

A versatile and commonly used stitch, the single crochet is abbreviated as SC. Due to its tight structure, it creates a dense fabric and is often the go-to stitch for amigurumi projects.

How to Single Crochet:

1. Insert the hook into the desired stitch.
2. Yarn over and pull up a loop.
3. Yarn over again and pull through both loops on the hook.

Double Crochet (DC):

Slightly taller than the single crochet, the double crochet is called DC. It adds height to your work and is frequently used for creating open and airy patterns.

How to Double Crochet:

1. Yarn over and insert the hook into the desired stitch.
2. Yarn over and pull up a loop.
3. Yarn over and pull through the first two loops on the hook.
4. Yarn over again and pull through the remaining two loops on the hook.

Half Double Crochet (HDC):

A mid-length stitch, the half-double crochet is abbreviated as HDC. It balances the single and double crochet, offering more height than the former.

How to Half Double Crochet:

1. Yarn over and insert the hook into the desired stitch.
2. Yarn over and pull up a loop.
3. Yarn over and pull through all three loops on the hook.

Treble Crochet (TR):

The treble crochet, abbreviated as TR, is a crucial stitch for projects requiring additional height. It creates a tall and open fabric, perfect for lacy designs.

How to Treble Crochet:

1. Yarn over twice and insert the hook into the desired stitch.
2. Yarn over and pull up a loop.
3. Yarn over and pull through the first two loops on the hook.
4. Yarn over and pull through the next two loops.
5. Yarn over again and pull through the remaining two loops on the hook.

Repeat (Rep):

When you encounter "rep" in a pattern, it signals that you should repeat the specified sequence of stitches or actions. The number of repetitions will be indicated, ensuring you create consistent patterns across your project.

Example: "SC in each stitch across, a rep for the next three rows."

Skip (Sk):

The skip instruction, abbreviated as "sk," directs you to pass over a specified number of stitches or chains without working into them and creates intentional spaces or gaps in your crochet fabric.

Example: "Skip the next two stitches, then DC in the following stitch."

In the Round (RND):

For projects working in a continuous spiral, the abbreviation "RND" indicates that you should work in a circular pattern without turning your work.

Example: "SC in each stitch around for RND 3."

Front Loop (FL) and Back Loop (BL):

Patterns may instruct you to work in a stitch's front loop (FL) or back loop (BL) for texture or design purposes. Understanding these terms adds versatility to your crochet skills.

Example: "HDC in the BL only for the next row."

Right Side (RS) and Wrong Side (WS):

Identifying the right side (RS) and wrong side (WS) of your work is crucial for achieving the intended design. The RS is often the side facing outward, while the WS may be hidden or used for seaming.

Example: "With the RS facing you, SC across."

Tips for Mastery:

1. **Create a Reference Sheet:** Keep a handy reference sheet with standard abbreviations

and their meanings. This personalized cheat sheet will be a quick guide when encountering unfamiliar terms.

2. **Practice Stitch Combinations:** Mastering basic stitches is foundational, but practice combining them to create intricate patterns will boost your confidence when tackling advanced projects.

3. **Join Crochet Communities:** Join online crochet communities to discuss abbreviations, seek advice, and share experiences. Engaging with a community provides valuable insights and support.

4. **Experiment with Stitch Variations:** As you become more comfortable with standard stitches, explore variations like front and back post stitches, cluster stitches, and more to broaden your repertoire and enhance your creativity.

5. **Embrace Lifelong Learning:** Crochet, like any craft, is continuously evolving. Stay open to learning new stitches and techniques, and embrace the joy of lifelong learning in crochet.

Mastering crochet abbreviations and terms is like learning a new language—one stitch at a time. You'll effortlessly translate patterns into beautiful amigurumi creations as you become fluent.

3.3 Special Stitch Techniques

While the foundation of crochet lies in basic stitches, delving into special stitches opens up a world of creativity and intricacy in your projects. This section will introduce you to several special stitches, providing detailed instructions and creative insights to elevate your crochet skills.

1. Popcorn Stitch:

Overview: The popcorn stitch adds delightful texture and dimension to your work, creating small, puffy clusters resembling popcorn. It's commonly used for decorative elements in blankets, hats, and amigurumi.

How to Popcorn:

1. Work the required number of stitches in the same stitch or space.
2. Remove the hook from the working loop.
3. Insert the hook from front to back into the first stitch of the group.
4. Catch the working loop with the hook and pull it through the stitch.

   Tip: Experiment with variations by working popcorn stitches of different heights or combining them in unique patterns.

2. Shell Stitch:

Overview: The shell stitch is a classic crochet technique that creates a fan-like pattern. It's versatile and often used for lacy edges, shawls, and decorative elements in amigurumi.

How to Shell Stitch:

1. Work the required number of stitches in the same stitch or space.
2. Chain one to create space.
3. Work the same number of stitches in the same stitch or space.
4. Repeat the sequence for subsequent shell stitches.

Tip: Adjust the shell size by varying the number of stitches and chains in each shell.

3. Picot Stitch:

Overview: Picots are small loops that add a delicate, decorative edge to your crochet work. They are commonly used in lace patterns and for creating intricate details in amigurumi.

How to Picot:

1. Chain a small number of stitches (typically 3 to 5).
2. Slip stitch into the first chain to create a loop.

Tip: Experiment with picot size to achieve different effects, and use picots to create loops for attaching embellishments.

4. Bobble Stitch:

Overview: The bobble stitch creates a raised, textured cluster of stitches. It's excellent for adding visual interest to your projects and can be used for various decorative elements.

How to Bobble:

1. Yarn over and insert the hook into the designated stitch.
2. Yarn over and pull up a loop.
3. Yarn over and pull through two loops on the hook (repeat this step for the specified number of times).
4. Yarn over and pull through all loops on the hook to close the bobble.

Tip: Experiment with bobble size by adjusting the number of loops and repetitions.

5. Crocodile Stitch:

Overview: The crocodile stitch creates a layered, scale-like pattern reminiscent of dragon scales. While often used in accessories, it can add a whimsical touch to amigurumi.

How to Crocodile Stitch:

1. Work a foundation row of chain stitches.
2. Work a sequence of stitches around the posts of the chain stitches, creating scales.

Tip: Combine different yarn colors for a vibrant and textured effect, resembling the scales of mythical creatures.

6. Front and Back Post Stitches:

Overview: Front and back post stitches create a raised ribbing effect, adding texture and structure to your work. They are commonly used in garments and accessories but can also enhance amigurumi designs.

How to Front and Back Post Stitches:

1. Yarn over and insert the hook around the post of the designated stitch from front to back (front post) or back to front (back post).
2. Complete the designated stitch as usual.

Tip: Combine front and back post stitches to create intricate cable patterns and three-dimensional textures.

Creative Insights:

1. **Mixing Special Stitches:** Combine special stitches in a single project to create unique textures and visual interest. For example, alternate rows of shell stitches with rows of bobbles for a captivating effect.
2. **Color Play:** Experiment with color changes within special stitches to highlight their unique patterns. Variegated yarns can add more complexity to your special stitch projects.
3. **Amigurumi Embellishments:** Use special stitches, such as textured flowers or decorative patches, to craft embellishments for your amigurumi. These details can bring your dolls to life with character and charm.

   Remember, special stitches are like artistic tools in your crochet toolkit. Feel free to explore, experiment, and incorporate them into your amigurumi projects to add a touch of individuality and flair.

3.4 Colorwork and Chart Reading

Colorwork is a captivating aspect of crochet that allows you to infuse your projects with personality, depth, and intricate patterns. This section will explore the fundamentals of changing colors, carrying yarn, and reading color charts. Whether creating elaborate tapestries or enhancing the charm of your amigurumi, mastering colorwork will elevate your crochet skills to new heights.

1. Changing Colors:

Why Change Colors: Changing colors in your crochet work opens up a world of creative possibilities. It allows you to incorporate intricate patterns, create striking contrasts, and add depth to your projects.

How to Change Colors:

1. **Final Stitch of Previous Color:** Complete the last stitch of the current color until you have two loops on the hook.
2. **Yarn Over with New Color:** Introduce the new color by laying it over the hook and pulling it through the two loops.
3. **Securing the Color Change:** Tighten the stitch with the new color to secure it in place.
4. **Continuing with the New Color:** Proceed with the new color as indicated in the pattern.

Tip: To maintain a tidy and secure color change, weave in the yarn tails as you work.

2. Carrying yarn:

Why Carry Yarn: Carrying yarn is used in colorwork projects where you transition between colors without cutting the yarn; it is handy when working on intricate patterns with multiple color changes in a row.

How to Carry Yarn:

1. **Float the Inactive Yarn:** When switching colors, let the inactive yarn float along the back of the stitches until you need it again.
2. **Twist Yarns to Avoid Gaps:** To prevent gaps in your work, twist the two yarns around each other at the color change points.

Tip: Avoid carrying yarn over long distances to maintain an even tension and prevent snagging.

3. Reading Color Charts:

Why Use Color Charts: Color charts represent a crochet pattern, using symbols or colors to denote different stitches. They provide a clear and concise way to understand complex colorwork patterns.

How to Read Color Charts:

1. **Understand Symbol Key:** Familiarize yourself with the symbol key provided in the pattern. It explains the meaning of each symbol or color used in the chart.
2. **Follow Row-by-Row:** Read the color chart from right to left (for right-handed crocheters) or left to right (for left-handed crocheters), following the row numbers

indicated.

3. **Stitch Placement:** Each square on the chart represents a stitch. Match the symbol or color in the chart to the corresponding stitch in your work.

Tip: Use a magnetic board or sticky notes to keep track of your progress on the chart, moving row by row.

4. Intarsia Method:

Overview: Intarsia is a colorwork technique that involves using separate balls of yarn for each color block. It's commonly used for creating detailed pictures or patterns in crochet.

How to Intarsia:

1. **Use Separate Yarn Balls:** Prepare separate balls of yarn for each color block in your pattern.

2. **Twist Yarns at Color Changes:** Twist the yarns around each other at the color change points to avoid gaps.

3. **Maintain Tension:** Keep an even tension as you switch colors to create a smooth fabric.

Tip: Intarsia allows for precise color placement, making it ideal for intricate designs like logos or characters in amigurumi.

Creative Insights:

1. **Experiment with Color Combinations:** Play with contrasting and complementary colors to discover unique color combinations that enhance the visual appeal of your amigurumi.

2. **Gradient Colorwork:** Create stunning gradient effects by transitioning between shades of the same color family. This technique adds depth and dimension to your projects.

3. **Incorporate Colorwork in Small Doses:** If you're new to colorwork, start with small sections in your amigurumi projects and practice without committing to an entire color-intensive piece.

4. **Colorwork in the Round:** When working in the round, carry the yarn up inside the project to minimize the number of ends to weave in.

Mastering colorwork and chart reading opens up a world of creative expression in your crochet projects. Whether embellishing your amigurumi with intricate details or creating vibrant tapestries, these techniques will empower you to bring your artistic visions to life.

3.5 Gauge and Tension

Gauge and tension are fundamental aspects of crochet that often make the difference between a beautifully crafted project and one that falls short of expectations. In this section, we'll delve into the significance of gauge, why it matters, and how to achieve and maintain the proper tension for your crochet projects.

1. Understanding Gauge:

What is Gauge: Gauge refers to the number of stitches and rows within a specified measurement. It acts as a guide to ensure that your crochet project matches the dimensions outlined in the pattern.

Why Gauge Matters: Achieving the correct gauge is crucial for several reasons:

- **Size Consistency:** It ensures that your project is the right size, especially in garments or when following a specific design.
- **Yarn and Hook Compatibility:** Different yarns and hooks can produce varying results. Gauge helps you select the appropriate combination for your project.
- **Pattern Accuracy:** Following the recommended gauge ensures that your stitches align with the pattern, guaranteeing the intended look and fit.

2. Measuring Gauge:

Tools for Measuring Gauge:

- **Crochet Hook:** Use the hook recommended in the pattern.
- **Yarn:** Choose the yarn specified in the pattern.
- **Ruler or Gauge Swatch:** Essential for accurate measurement.

Creating a Gauge Swatch:

1. **Select Yarn and Hook:** Choose the yarn and hook mentioned in the pattern. If your natural tension differs, adjust accordingly.
2. **Crochet a Swatch:** Create a square swatch larger than the recommended gauge size. Use the main stitch pattern outlined in the instructions.
3. **Measure the Swatch:** Lay the swatch flat and use a ruler to count the number of stitches and rows within the specified dimensions. Measure in the center to minimize distortion.
4. **Adjust as Needed:** Adjust your hook size accordingly if your swatch doesn't match the pattern's gauge.
   - **Too Many Stitches/Rows:** Switch to a larger hook.
   - **Too Few Stitches/Rows:** Switch to a smaller hook.

3. Achieving Proper Tension:

Why Tension Matters: Tension is the amount of pressure applied to the yarn as you crochet. Consistent tension ensures that your stitches are uniform, creating an aesthetically pleasing and well-finished project.

Tips for Maintaining Tension:

1. **Relaxed Grip:** Hold the hook comfortably without gripping too tightly. A comfortable grip promotes even tension.

2. **Consistent Yarn Feed:** Pull the yarn consistently for each stitch. Avoid erratic pulling, which can lead to uneven tension.

3. **Practice Regularly:** Tension often improves with practice. Crochet regularly to build muscle memory and achieve a more consistent stitch.

4. **Evaluate tension Periodically:** Pause and assess your tension as you crochet. Adjust if you notice variations in stitch size.

5. **Be Mindful of Stress:** External factors like stress can impact tension—Crochet in a relaxed environment to maintain consistent results.

Creative Insights:

1. **Gauge Variations for Different Projects:** Understand that different projects may require adjustments in gauge. For example, a blanket may allow more flexibility than a fitted garment.

2. **Blocking for Gauge Corrections:** Blocking your finished project can help correct minor gauge discrepancies. However, it's essential to prioritize achieving the correct gauge during the crocheting process.

3. **Experiment with Tension Styles:** Some crocheters naturally have a looser or tighter tension. Experiment with different tension styles to find what works best for you.

4. **Swatch for Complex Patterns:** For intricate patterns or projects where fit is crucial, create a larger swatch that includes various stitches to ensure accuracy.

Understanding and mastering gauge and tension will empower you to approach your crochet projects and achieve professional-looking results. Consistency in these foundational elements is key to turning your creative visions into beautifully crafted realities.

3.6 Tips for Efficient Crocheting

Crocheting is not just a craft; it's a joyful journey. This section will share practical tips and techniques to enhance your crochet experience, making your sessions more enjoyable and productive. From organizing your materials to optimizing your workspace, these efficiency hacks will elevate your crocheting to a new level of satisfaction.

1. Organizing Your Oasis: Creating a Crochet-Friendly Space

- **Designate a Dedicated Space:** Create a specific area for your crochet endeavors. Whether a cozy corner or an entire room, having a designated space fosters creativity and helps organize your materials.

- **Invest in Storage Solutions:** Utilize storage containers, shelves, and baskets to keep yarn, hooks, and other essentials neatly arranged. Transparent containers make it easy to identify colors and textures.

- **Organize by Color or Project:** Sort your yarn by color or group materials based on ongoing projects; it adds visual appeal and streamlines your creative process.

- **Comfortable Seating:** Invest in a comfortable chair or seating arrangement. Proper support reduces fatigue during longer crochet sessions.

- **Good Lighting:** Ensure ample lighting in your crochet space. Natural light is ideal, but opt for bright, white LED lights to reduce eye strain if impossible.

2. Time-Saving Techniques: Streamlining Your Crochet Process

- **The Magic Ring for Seamless Starts:** Master the magic ring (adjustable ring) for starting projects seamlessly. This technique provides a tight, closed center for amigurumi and other circular projects.

- **Seamless Color Changes:** Learn to change colors seamlessly without knots or visible transitions. This technique is handy for projects with intricate color patterns.

- **Yarn Management:** Organize multiple yarn skeins or colors in a bowl or holder to prevent tangling and ensure a smooth crocheting experience.

- **Utilize Stitch Markers:** Employ stitch markers to highlight specific points in your pattern. They're invaluable for marking the beginning of a round, indicating stitch changes, or highlighting key locations.

- **Weaving in Ends as You Go:** Avoid weaving in numerous ends at the end of a project. Weave in yarn tails as you crochet to maintain a clean and organized final piece.

3. Comfort and Ergonomics: Prioritizing Your Well-being

- **Ergonomic Hooks and Tools:** Invest in ergonomic crochet hooks to reduce strain on your hands and wrists. Cushioned handles provide comfort during extended crochet sessions.

- **Take Breaks:** Take short breaks to stretch your hands and shoulders to prevent stiffness and discomfort, promoting a healthier crochet experience.
- **Posture Awareness:** Maintain good posture while crocheting. Sit in a way that supports your back and shoulders to prevent long-term strain.
- **Hand Exercises:** Incorporate hand exercises into your routine to maintain flexibility and strength. Simple stretches and movements can significantly benefit your hand health.

4. Creative Insights:

- **Personalizing Your Space:** Decorate your crochet space with items that inspire you, such as handmade decor, inspirational quotes, or photos. A personalized space enhances your connection to the craft.
- **Experimenting with Hook Grips:** Try different grips for your crochet hook to find the one that suits you best. Pencil grip, knife grip, and other variations offer diverse ergonomic options.
- **Customizing Techniques:** Feel free to adapt techniques to fit your style. Crocheting is a creative journey, and customizing certain aspects can enhance your enjoyment of the craft.
- **Mindful Crocheting:** Engage in mindful crocheting by focusing on each stitch and embracing the meditative quality of the craft to enhance your crochet experience and reduce stress.

Crafting is not just about the end product; it's about the journey—the stitches, the colors, and the sense of accomplishment with each completed project. In this chapter, we've unlocked the crochet language, providing the tools to read patterns, master abbreviations, explore special stitches, and understand colorwork and gauge. We've also delved into tips and techniques to make your crochet sessions more efficient and enjoyable.

Remember, each stitch is a step forward in your creative adventure. Embrace the learning process, celebrate the quirks, and revel in the joy of bringing your imagination to life.

Chapter 4: Crochet Materials

4.1 Yarn Variety and Selection

Welcome to the enchanting world of yarn, where every fiber holds a story waiting to be spun. In this section, we'll delve deeper into the intricate details of yarn, exploring its diverse weights, fibers, and the magic of color that brings your amigurumi to life.

Yarn weight is the heartbeat of your crochet project, determining its texture, drape, and overall aesthetic. Let's journey through the spectrum of yarn weights, from the delicate whisper of lace to the bold jumbo statement.

- **Lace Weight:** Delicate as a dream, lace-weight yarn is perfect for intricate details and lightweight creations. Dive into the world of ethereal shawls and delicate amigurumi accessories.
- **Fingering Weight:** Often used for delicate garments, fingering weight yarn is versatile and offers a fine texture. Explore its use in creating charming amigurumi with intricate patterns and detailed features.
- **Sport Weight:** A balance of fine texture and substance, sport-weight yarn is ideal for creating well-defined stitches. Discover its charm in crafting adorable amigurumi garments with a touch of sophistication.
- **Worsted Weight:** The workhorse of yarn weights, worsted weight, is perfect for various projects, including sturdy amigurumi dolls with a plush feel.
- **Bulky and Jumbo Weight:** Make a statement with bulky and jumbo weight yarn, creating huggable amigurumi with a cozy, chunky appeal.

Understanding these weights empowers you to choose the perfect yarn for your amigurumi vision, ensuring it aligns with your desired texture and appearance.

Like every character has a distinct personality, every yarn fiber brings unique characteristics to your amigurumi creations. Let's explore the magical world of yarn fibers, guiding you to choose the perfect thread for your specific vision.

- **Acrylic:** Vibrant and affordable, acrylic yarn offers various colors. It's a fantastic choice for creating dolls with bold, expressive features.
- **Cotton:** cotton yarn is breathable and ideal for crafting amigurumi with a soft, matte finish. Explore its use in creating dolls with a natural and classic appeal.
- **Wool:** Embrace warmth and texture with wool yarn. Perfect for cozy amigurumi

companions, wool adds a fuzzy, huggable quality to your dolls.

- **Blends:** Combine the best of different worlds with yarn blends. Explore the characteristics of acrylic-wool blends, cotton-bamboo blends, and more. Blends offer versatility, durability, and a unique texture.

Choosing the suitable fiber allows you to tailor your amigurumi's feel, appearance, and care requirements, ensuring each doll is a distinct work of art.

Color is the language of crochet, and your amigurumi's palette is its voice. Let's unlock the secrets of color theory, understanding how hues, tones, and shades influence your dolls' mood and visual appeal.

- **Primary Colors:** Dive into the basics of color theory, exploring the impact of primary colors on your amigurumi. Understand how these colors can be combined to create a vibrant and lively palette.
- **Complementary Colors:** Discover the magic of complementary colors, creating striking contrasts that bring energy and visual interest to your dolls.
- **Analogous Colors:** Explore the subtle harmony of matching colors, crafting dolls with a soothing and cohesive color scheme.
- **Monochromatic Colors:** Embrace the simplicity and elegance of monochromatic color schemes. Learn how a single color can create depth and sophistication in your amigurumi.

With a deep understanding of color theory, you'll be equipped to choose colors that resonate with your creative vision, making each amigurumi a masterpiece of expression.

In the intricate dance of yarn weights, fibers, and colors, your amigurumi takes shape as a unique creation. As you explore the endless possibilities, remember that each thread holds the potential to weave dreams into reality, one stitch at a time.

4.2 The Crochet Hook Chronicles

In the enchanted realm of crochet, the hook is your magic wand—a tool that transforms yarn into whimsical creations. In this section, let's delve into the profound artistry of the crochet hook, unraveling its anatomy, materials, and the secrets it holds.

A crochet hook, seemingly simple, is a complex conductor of creativity. Understanding its anatomy is crucial for choosing the right crochet journey tool.

- **Throat:** The throat of the hook determines how easily it can glide through stitches. A tapered throat suits tight stitches, while a more bottomless throat accommodates bulkier yarn.

- **Shaft:** The shaft bridges the throat and the hook's working end. The length and thickness of the shaft influence stitch size and tension.
- **Handle:** the handle is at the opposite end of the hook from the working end and is your control point. It comes in various shapes and sizes to cater to different preferences.
- **Working End:** The hook features a point and a groove. The point inserts into stitches, and the groove holds the yarn securely. The size and shape of the working end affect stitch appearance and ease of use.

Crochet hooks, crafted from various materials, offer a spectrum of tactile experiences. Delve into hook materials to discover the one that aligns with your comfort and crocheting rhythm.

- **Aluminum:** Lightweight and affordable, aluminum hooks are a popular choice. They offer a smooth surface for easy stitching and are suitable for various yarn types.
- **Steel:** Often used for delicate projects and fine threads, steel hooks are durable and maintain their shape well.
- **Wood:** Wooden hooks provide warmth and a comfortable grip. They are suitable for those who prefer a slower stitching pace.
- **Ergonomic Options:** Ergonomic hooks feature handles for comfort during extended crocheting sessions. These handles may be made of rubber, silicone, or other soft materials to reduce strain.

Choosing the suitable material is a personal journey, influenced by the feel in your hand and the rhythm of your stitches. Explore different materials to find the one that enhances your crochet experience.

Deciphering hook sizes is akin to reading a secret code; each size unlocks possibilities. Master the art of understanding hook sizes, ensuring you select the appropriate wand for your chosen yarn and project.

- **Millimeters:** The most precise measurement indicates the diameter of the hook's shaft.
- **Numbers:** Numeric sizing is standard in the United States. The higher the number, the smaller the hook.
- **Letters:** Letter sizing is also used in the U.S., with more giant letters indicating smaller hooks.

Understanding these sizing conventions empowers you to match your hook to your project's demands, creating just the right stitches.

As you embark on your amigurumi adventure, consider the crochet hook your steadfast companion—a partner in creating charming dolls. The anatomy, material, and size of your hook contribute to the unique personality of each stitch, guiding you through a magical dance with yarn. May your hooks be swift and your creations enchanting.

4.3 Notions and Accessories Extravaganza

Welcome to the enchanting world beyond yarn and hook—a realm where notions and accessories become the supporting characters in your crochet tale. In this section, we'll unravel the mysteries of these tools, exploring their utility and the magic they bring to your amigurumi creations.

Like guiding stars, stitch markers are crucial in keeping your crochet journey on course. These tiny tools come in various forms, each serving a unique purpose.

- **Ring Markers:** Circular markers that slide onto your hook or stitches, helping you keep track of the beginning of rounds or specific stitches.
- **Locking Markers:** These markers clip onto stitches, making them versatile for various stitch counts, color changes, or pattern repeats.
- **Split Ring Markers:** Similar to ring markers but with an opening, allowing you to place or remove them without disrupting your stitches.

Choosing the right stitch marker depends on your project's needs. They are your navigators in the yarn sea, ensuring smooth sailing through intricate patterns and color changes.

Yarn and tapestry needles are the weavers of your yarn tales, seamlessly blending ends, attaching limbs, and adding intricate details.

- **Yarn Needles:** Straight needles with a large eye, ideal for weaving in yarn ends and sewing together crocheted pieces.
- **Tapestry Needles:** Blunt-tipped needles with a giant eye, perfect for working with yarn and creating decorative stitches.

Mastering the art of weaving is a skill every amigurumi enthusiast should embrace. These needles bring cohesion to your creations, ensuring each stitch tells a harmonious story.

In the architectural realm of crochet, accuracy is paramount. Measuring tools are the architects, ensuring your amigurumi follows the blueprint precisely.

- **Measuring Tapes:** Flexible and ideal for measuring your finished or in-progress projects.
- **Rulers:** Sturdy and perfect for checking gauges and measuring small components.

As you venture into the world of notions and accessories, consider them as allies, enhancing your crochet experience. Stitch markers guide you, needles weave your story, and measuring tools ensure precision in every stitch. Together, they transform your crochet from a craft into an art form. May your notions be ever at hand, and your accessories add flair to your creations.

4.4 Safety Eyes and Embellishments

In the magical world of amigurumi, safety eyes are the windows to the soul, and embellishments are the intricate details that breathe life into your creations. Let's delve into adding expressive features and charming flourishes to your amigurumi dolls.

Safety eyes and noses are the keys to giving your amigurumi characters distinct personalities. These features add charm and ensure durability and safety, especially if your creations are for young ones.

- **Choosing the Right Size:** Safety eyes come in various sizes, typically measured in millimeters. Consider the size of your amigurumi and the expression you want to achieve. More enormous eyes often convey innocence, while smaller ones create a more focused or mischievous look.
- **Securing Safety Eyes:** To securely attach safety eyes, decide on their placement. Push the eye through the stitch from the outside, add the washer from the inside, and snap it into place, ensuring a snug fit that withstands hugs and plays.
- **Noses for Character:** Safety noses, often used with safety eyes, come in different shapes. Triangle-shaped noses suit an animal character, while round ones are perfect for a whimsical creature. Attach them firmly, ensuring they complement the facial expression.

Understanding the nuances of safety eyes and noses empowers you to create amigurumi dolls with distinct characters and expressions.

Embroidery threads are the artist's brush, adding intricate details and personal touches to your amigurumi. From facial expressions to patterns and embellishments, embroidery threads open a realm of creative possibilities.

- **Choosing the Right Thread:** Select embroidery threads that complement your yarn in color and thickness. Thinner threads suit delicate details, while thicker ones add bold accents.
- **Facial Expressions:** Embroider eyes, eyebrows, and mouths to convey a range of emotions. Experiment with different stitch styles, such as satin for smooth surfaces and

backstitch for outlines.

- **Patterns and Embellishments:** Use embroidery to create patterns on clothing or add decorative elements to your amigurumi. Flowers, swirls, and other embellishments can transform a plain doll into a work of art.

Embroidery threads are your tools for personalization, allowing you to infuse your amigurumi with unique character and style.

Elevate your amigurumi from charming to enchanting with decorative accessories. Ribbons, buttons, and charms are the finishing touches that make your creations unique.

- **Crafting Garments:** Create miniature garments like dresses, hats, and scarves to adorn your amigurumi. Choose colors and textures that complement the doll's personality.
- **Button Embellishments:** Sew buttons onto clothing or directly onto the doll to add a touch of whimsy. Different shapes, sizes, and colors offer endless possibilities.
- **Charming Charms:** Attach small charms to a doll's hand or around its neck for a delightful and personalized touch. Consider charms that reflect the theme or story of your amigurumi.

Incorporating safety eyes and embellishments is where your amigurumi truly comes to life. These details transform a simple crocheted doll into a cherished companion, brimming with personality and charm. As you navigate this section, let your creativity flow, and watch as your amigurumi takes on its character.

4.5 Storage and Organization Strategies

Welcome to the realm of order and creativity—a place where your yarn stash is not a chaotic jungle but a curated collection ready to inspire your next masterpiece. Let's explore adequate storage and organization strategies that turn your crafting space into a haven of creativity.

Your yarn is a palette of possibilities, and organizing it keeps your space tidy and sparks inspiration. Consider these storage solutions to maintain the vibrancy and accessibility of your yarn collection:

- **Shelving Systems:** Install open shelving units to neatly arrange your yarn by color, weight, or project to create an aesthetically pleasing display that allows you to identify and grab the yarn you need.
- **Clear Containers:** Invest in transparent containers to store yarn for a visual feast of colors while protecting your yarn from dust and potential damage. Label each container to

locate the specific yarn you're searching for quickly.

- **Yarn Bowls:** Decorative and functional, yarn bowls keep your working yarn clean and prevent tangles. They are an elegant addition to your workspace, offering a touch of craftsmanship and artistry.

Keeping your tools and works-in-progress organized is essential for the crocheter on the move or someone with multiple ongoing projects. Here's how you can do it:

- **Hook Cases:** Invest in a hook case with compartments for different hook sizes to keep your hooks in order and prevent them from getting lost or damaged. Some cases even include additional pockets for accessories like stitch markers.

- **Project Bags:** Every project deserves its bag. Choose bags with pockets for your yarn, hooks, and other accessories. This way, you can easily pick up your project and continue crocheting wherever you go.

- **Labeling and Inventory:** Establish a labeling system for your yarn containers and project bags. It would be as simple as using tags or labels with details like yarn weight, color, and project name. An inventory helps you track your yarn stash and ongoing projects.

Only some have the luxury of a dedicated crafting room, but that should be fine with your creativity. Maximize small spaces with these clever ideas:

- **Hanging Organizers:** Utilize wall space by installing hanging organizers. These can hold yarn, hooks, and other accessories, keeping them within reach without taking up floor space.

- **Under-Bed Storage:** It's a discreet way to store yarn and works-in-progress to invest in storage containers that fit under your bed space, especially if space is at a premium.

- **Mobile Carts:** A rolling cart with multiple tiers is a versatile storage solution. Moving it around as needed provides ample space for yarn, tools, and works-in-progress.

By implementing these storage and organization strategies, you're not just keeping things in order but creating an environment that nurtures your creativity. A well-organized space allows you to focus on the joy of crocheting rather than searching for misplaced tools or yarn. Consider the unique aspects of your space and craft a system that suits your needs.

4.6 Sustainable and Eco-Friendly Options

Consider your craft's environmental impact as you embark on your amigurumi adventure. In this section, we'll explore sustainable and eco-friendly options that allow you to create beautiful dolls while minimizing your ecological footprint.

The yarn you choose can be a powerful decision that aligns with environmentally conscious practices. Here's a look at sustainable yarn options:

- **Recycled Yarn:** Crafted from post-consumer or post-industrial recycled fibers, recycled yarn repurposes materials that would otherwise end up in landfills. This option not only reduces waste but also gives a new life to existing fibers.

- **Organic Fibers:** Yarn from organic fibers, such as organic cotton or bamboo, is cultivated without synthetic pesticides or fertilizers. Choosing organic fibers supports sustainable agricultural practices.

- **Bamboo Yarn:** Bamboo is a fast-growing and renewable resource. Yarn made from bamboo fibers is soft, breathable, and eco-friendly. Bamboo plantations contribute to oxygen production and soil health.

Extend your commitment to sustainability beyond yarn by considering biodegradable accessories for your amigurumi:

- **Wooden Buttons:** Opt for wooden buttons instead of plastic ones. Wooden buttons are not only aesthetically pleasing but also biodegradable. They add a touch of natural charm to your dolls.

- **Biodegradable Stitch Markers:** Explore stitch markers made from wood, bamboo, or recycled paper. These markers are kind to the environment and can be composted at the end of their life cycle.

- **Natural Fiber Ribbons:** When adding decorative elements to your amigurumi, choose ribbons made from natural fibers like cotton or jute. These fibers break down naturally, contributing to a sustainable crafting cycle.

In addition to choosing sustainable materials, adopting mindful crafting practices reduces waste and promotes more eco-friendly approach:

- **Minimize Scrap Yarn:** Plan your projects to minimize scrap yarn. Use leftover yarn for smaller projects or incorporate scrap yarn into multi-colored designs.

- **Upcycling:** Get creative by using fabric scraps or old clothing to create unique outfits for your amigurumi to reduce waste and add a personal touch to your creations.

- **Environmentally Friendly Dyes:** If you enjoy dyeing your yarn, explore natural dyeing techniques with plant-based dyes to reduce the environmental impact of chemical dyes.

Crafting with consciousness adds a meaningful layer to your amigurumi journey. By making informed choices about your materials and embracing eco-friendly practices, you contribute to a more sustainable and environmentally friendly crafting community. Your dolls become charming creations and ambassadors for a greener, more mindful approach to crafting.

4.7 DIY Crafting Tools

In the world of amigurumi, creativity knows no bounds. Embrace the spirit of uniqueness and personalization by crafting your tools. This section explores how you can go beyond store-bought supplies and infuse your crafting sessions with a handmade charm.

Stitch markers are essential for keeping track of your rounds and stitches, but they can also be delightful accessories to showcase your personality. Here's how you can create your own:

- **Beaded Elegance:** Combine functionality with elegance by crafting beaded stitch markers. Choose beads in different colors and sizes to add a touch of flair to your markers. Use jewelry-making wire to secure the beads in a loop, creating a functional and aesthetically pleasing marker.

- **Polymer Clay Wonders:** Unleash your sculpting skills using polymer clay to create custom stitch markers. Mold tiny shapes or figures that resonate with the theme of your amigurumi project. Once baked, these markers become unique, miniature works of art.

- **Crocheted Charms:** If you love crocheting, extend your skills to create small charms that can serve as stitch markers. Experiment with different crochet motifs and colors to match the personality of your amigurumi dolls.

A yarn bowl is a practical accessory and a canvas for your artistic expression. Crafting your yarn bowl adds a personal touch to your crochet sessions:

- **Clay Creations:** Use air-dry or oven-bake clay to sculpt a bowl that suits your style. You can keep it simple and smooth or add intricate patterns and textures. The curved bowl prevents your yarn from rolling away while providing a visually pleasing container.

- **Upcycled Elegance:** Repurpose old containers or bowls to create unique yarn bowls. Paint or decorate them to match your crafting space or the theme of your current project. This eco-friendly approach gives new life to unused items.

- **Decoupage Delights:** Explore the art of decoupage by decorating a plain bowl with paper cutouts or fabric. Seal the design with decoupage glue for a polished finish. Your yarn bowl becomes a collage of your crafting journey.

Crafting your tools adds a personal touch to your crochet sessions and allows you to tailor them to your unique preferences. Whether you make elegant stitch markers or functional yarn bowls, the DIY approach turns your crafting space into a haven of creativity. Enjoy the process of crafting tools as much as you enjoy bringing your amigurumi dolls to life!

Chapter 5: Instructions for Crocheting

Welcome to the heart of amigurumi creation, where stitches transform into whimsical characters. This chapter guides you to mastering the fundamental techniques that breathe life into enchanting amigurumi dolls. Whether you're a novice or an experienced crocheter, these step-by-step instructions will empower you to create your own charming and unique dolls.

5.1 Basic Amigurumi Shapes

1. Creating a Magic Ring (Adjustable Ring)

The magic ring, also known as the adjustable ring, is crucial for starting many amigurumi projects. This technique provides a seamless and tight beginning, ensuring your dolls have a polished and professional look.

Let's break down the steps:

- Hold the yarn tail: Before you begin, hold the yarn tail securely between your thumb and middle finger to ensure stability as you work the initial stitches.

- Make a loop with the working yarn: Cross the working yarn over the yarn tail to create a loop. The working yarn should be on top.

- Insert the hook through the loop: With the loop in place, insert your crochet hook from front to back under the loop. Ensure that both the tail and working yarn are behind the hook.

- Pull up a loop and chain one: Yarn over with the working yarn and pull up a loop through the loop to create a slipknot. Chain one to secure the ring, making it adjustable for tightening later.

- Proceed with the first round: Now that the magic ring is formed, you can work the first round of stitches directly into the ring. Be mindful of the tension, pulling the tail to close the circle as you complete your stitches.

Tips for Success:

- Practice this technique with scrap yarn until you feel comfortable.
- Adjust the tightness of the ring by pulling the tail after completing the first round.
- Some patterns might use alternative methods, but the magic ring is favored for its clean and tight appearance.

2. Single Crochet Stitch

The single crochet stitch is the fundamental building block of amigurumi. It creates a sturdy and compact fabric that maintains the doll's shape.

Let's explore the steps:

- Insert the hook into the stitch: Identify the stitch you want to work into. Insert your crochet hook from front to back under both stitch loops.
- Yarn over and pull up a loop: Wrap the working yarn over the hook (yarn over) and pull it back through the stitch. You now have two loops on the hook.
- Yarn over again and pull through both loops on the hook: Complete the single crochet by yarn over again and pulling it through both loops on the hook to leave you with one loop on the hook.

Tips for Success:

- Maintain a consistent tension to create an even and neat fabric.
- Practice the single crochet stitch on a small swatch before starting your amigurumi project.
- Use the correct hook size for your yarn to achieve the desired tightness.

3. Increasing and Decreasing

Understanding how to increase and decrease stitches is crucial for shaping your amigurumi. These techniques control the number of stitches in a round and influence the overall form of your doll.

Increasing:

- To increase, work two single crochets in the same stitch and create an additional stitch, expanding the circumference of your project. Increases are often used when shaping rounded sections like heads and bodies.

Decreasing:

- To decrease, combine two stitches into one. This technique reduces the number of stitches, creating a narrower or tapered section. Decreases are expected when shaping limbs or creating a pointed base.

Tips for Success:

- Follow the pattern instructions for the placement of increases and decreases.
- Use stitch markers to highlight where increases or decreases should occur.
- Practice these techniques on a small swatch to visualize how they impact the fabric.

Mastering these basic amigurumi shapes sets the stage for creating various characters and designs. Practice each step, and soon, you'll confidently navigate the magic ring, single crochet stitch, and shaping techniques, bringing your amigurumi visions to life!

5.2 Shaping and Sculpting

4. Shaping Techniques for Limbs

One of the joys of crafting amigurumi is the ability to infuse personality and vitality into your creations. Achieving lifelike and well-defined limbs requires careful shaping techniques. Let's delve into the essential steps:

Creating Limbs:

1. **Shape Arms and Legs Separately Before Attaching:** When crafting amigurumi dolls, it's often beneficial to shape arms and legs as separate pieces before attaching them to the body. This approach provides more control over the limbs' size, length, and positioning.

2. **Use Stitch Markers for Precision:** Employ stitch markers to indicate your limbs' starting and ending points to ensure consistency and symmetry in your design.

Incorporating Curves:

1. **Strategic Use of Increases and Decreases:** To achieve curved features like rounded arms and legs, strategically place increases and decreases. For example, to create a tapered effect, increase at the start of the limb and decrease towards the end.

2. **Experiment with Stitch Count:** Play around with the stitch count in each round to experiment with different shapes. Increasing in certain rounds and maintaining a consistent stitch count in others allows for a variety of limb shapes.

5. Adding Facial Features

The facial features of your amigurumi doll are where its unique character comes to life. Mastering the art of facial features involves precision and creativity. Here's how you can achieve expressive and charming faces:

Embroidering Eyes and Mouth:

1. **Utilize Embroidery Techniques:** Embroidery is a versatile and accessible method for creating eyes and mouths. Use a yarn needle and embroidery thread to stitch eyes and a mouth carefully onto the face.

2. **Experiment with Stitch Placement:** The placement of stitches contributes to the expression of your amigurumi. Play with the distance between stitches to achieve different emotions, from wide-eyed innocence to a subtle smirk.

Attaching Safety Eyes:

1. **Secure and Polished Look:** Safety eyes provide a polished and fast way to add a professional finish to your amigurumi. These eyes come in various sizes and colors, allowing for customization based on your doll's personality.

2. **Follow Pattern Instructions:** When using safety eyes, follow the pattern instructions for placement. Use the included washers to secure the eyes, ensuring they stay in place.

5.3 Clothing and Accessories

6. Designing Doll Clothing

Adding clothing and accessories to your amigurumi takes them to the next level, allowing for personalization and style. Here's how you can craft miniature garments for your dolls:

Creating Garments:

1. **Select Appropriate Yarn and Hook:** Choose a yarn weight and hook size that complements the size of your amigurumi doll and ensure that the clothing fits well and has the desired drape.

2. **Follow Garment Patterns:** Use garment patterns designed for amigurumi. These patterns often include instructions for shaping and sizing, making it easier to create a perfect fit.

Adding Details:

1. **Buttons, Bows, and Decorative Elements:** Enhance your doll's clothing with buttons, bows, and other decorative elements. These details add flair and personality to your amigurumi.

2. **Explore Embellishment Techniques:** Experiment with embellishment techniques such as surface crochet or appliqué to add intricate details to the clothing.

7. Accessory Attachments

Amigurumi accessories are the finishing touches that make your dolls genuinely unique. From tiny bags to scarves and hats, accessories allow for endless customization.

1. **Choose Complementary Colors:** Select colors for accessories that complement the overall color scheme of your amigurumi to create a cohesive and stylish look.

2. **Scale Accessories Appropriately:** Consider the size of your amigurumi when crafting accessories. Tiny dolls benefit from smaller accessories to maintain proportion.

3. **Weave in Ends for Durability:** Attach accessories securely by weaving in ends to ensure that accessories stay in place during play and display.

4. **Follow Pattern Recommendations:** If using a pattern for accessories, follow the recommended attachment methods to ensure a professional and durable finish.

5.4 Advanced Techniques

8. Colorwork and Intarsia

Advanced techniques like colorwork and intarsia allow you to create intricate and colorful designs within your amigurumi.

1. **Seamless Transitions:** Learn how to transition between yarn colors seamlessly. This skill is crucial for creating multicolored designs without visible joins.

2. **Experiment with Color Placement:** Play with color placement to create patterns, stripes, or other visual effects to add sophistication to your amigurumi.

3. **Creating Detailed Patterns:** Master the art of intarsia, which involves knitting or crocheting blocks of color to create detailed patterns. This technique is ideal for adding complex designs to your amigurumi.

4. **Follow Intarsia Charts:** If using a pattern, follow the provided intarsia charts for accurate color placement to ensure your intricate designs turn out as intended.

9. Incorporating Wire Armatures

Take your amigurumi to the next level by incorporating internal wire armatures to make your dolls poseable and add an extra element of creativity.

1. **Mold a Wire Skeleton:** Use pliable wire to create a skeleton that fits within your doll, provides structure, and allows for possibility.

2. **Covering with Fiber:** Cover the wire skeleton with fiber, such as crochet stitches, and add a layer of safety to create a seamless and polished appearance.

3. **Secure Attachment for Flexibility:** Attach the limbs to the wire skeleton securely to ensure that the limbs are flexible and hold the desired pose.

4. **Experiment with Poses:** Once the wire armature is in place, experiment with different poses for your amigurumi to add a dynamic and playful element to your creations.

Mastering these crochet techniques will empower you to bring your amigurumi visions to life. Follow each step confidently, and soon, you'll create your own charming and unique dolls.

Chapter 6: Techniques and Tips

Welcome to the realm of advanced crochet techniques and invaluable tips that will elevate your craftsmanship. In this chapter, we'll delve into the intricacies of stitching, offering a treasure trove of skills and insights to enhance your crochet journey. Whether you want to refine your stitches, troubleshoot common challenges, or experiment with innovative methods, this comprehensive guide is your passport to crochet mastery.

6.1 Mastering Stitch Variations

1. Bobble Stitch Brilliance:

The bobble stitch is a fascinating addition to your crochet repertoire, bringing texture and character to your creations. Understanding its variations allows you to tailor its use to different projects.

- **Classic Bobble:** The traditional bobble creates a cluster of stitches in the same stitch or space, giving a rounded and puffy appearance. Experiment with the number of stitches in the cluster for varying sizes.
- **Textured Puff Stitch:** Enhance your bobble game by exploring the textured puff stitch. This variation introduces additional yarnovers, creating a more intricate and visually appealing texture.
- **Cluster Bobble:** Combine the bobble with cluster stitches to achieve a unique and denser texture. This variation is excellent for projects where you want a pronounced, raised effect.

2. Cable Crochet Techniques:

Cable crochet adds an elegant touch, mimicking the classic look of knitted cables. Mastering this technique opens up new possibilities for creating sophisticated and visually exciting patterns.

- **Front Post and Back Post Stitches:** Cables are formed by working front post and back post stitches. Understand the difference between these stitches to create the twisting effect characteristic of cables.
- **Crossed Cables:** Experiment with crossed cable stitches, which are worked out of order, crossing over each other. This technique adds complexity and depth to your crochet projects.
- **Interlocking Cables:** Take cable crochet to the next level by interlocking cables, creating

intricate designs that intertwine seamlessly. This technique is ideal for advanced projects like blankets or garments.

3. Lacework Wonders:

Lace crochet brings a delicate and airy quality to your projects. Mastering lacework allows you to create intricate and visually stunning patterns.

- **Openwork Mesh:** Explore the basics of openwork mesh, where chains and double crochets create a breathable and lightweight fabric. Adjusting the spacing provides versatility in your lace designs.

- **Pineapple Stitch:** Dive into the intricacies of the pineapple stitch, a classic lace pattern resembling the tropical fruit. This stitch is perfect for shawls, doilies, and other decorative items.

- **Filet Crochet:** Combine lace and charts in filet crochet. Learn to read and follow charts to create intricate designs, making this technique suitable for projects ranging from tablecloths to wall hangings.

Understanding these variations within each stitch category empowers you to choose the proper technique for your project, adding depth, texture, and sophistication to your crochet creations.

6.2 Troubleshooting Challenges

Crocheting is a delightful journey, but challenges may arise along the way. Fear not! Let's delve into everyday issues and equip you with the knowledge to troubleshoot and overcome them, ensuring a smooth and enjoyable crochet experience.

1. Uneven Tension

Achieving consistent tension is fundamental to a polished project. Uneven tension can result in a crooked or misshapen creation. Here's how to address it:

- Practice regular tension exercises to enhance control.
- Pay attention to your grip on the yarn and hook; a relaxed grip promotes even tension.
- Experiment with different yarn-holding methods until you find one that suits you.

2. Dropped Stitches

Dropped stitches can lead to holes in your fabric and disrupt the overall pattern. Early catching them prevents unraveling. Tips:

- Count stitches regularly to catch any discrepancies.

- Use stitch markers to denote specific points, making it easier to identify dropped stitches.
- If a stitch drops, use a crochet hook or needle to pick it up before it unravels further.

3. Twisted Chains

A twisted starting chain can affect the entire project's alignment and appearance. Fortunately, it's easily preventable. Tips:

- Lay the foundation chain flat as you crochet to avoid twists.
- Periodically check that the chain is straight before continuing.

4. Difficulty in Reading Patterns

Interpreting crochet patterns can be challenging, especially for beginners. Let's demystify this process. Tips:

- Familiarize yourself with standard crochet abbreviations.
- Read through the pattern before starting to identify potential stumbling blocks.
- Break down complex instructions into smaller, manageable steps.

5. Yarn Tangling

Yarn tangling can be frustrating and disrupt your flow. Addressing this issue ensures a smoother crochet session. Tips:

- Use a yarn bowl or dispenser to prevent excessive yarn movement.
- Detangle yarn as you work rather than waiting for a significant knot to form.
- Choose the suitable yarn storage method based on the yarn type and project.

6. Inconsistent Stitch Size

Maintaining consistent stitch size is crucial for an even fabric. Inconsistencies may result in an irregular surface. Tips:

- Pay attention to your tension and gauge throughout the project.
- Use stitch markers to denote specific points to maintain consistency.

Arming yourself with troubleshooting skills enhances your confidence and enjoyment of crocheting. Remember, each challenge is an opportunity to refine your skills and create something beautiful.

6.3 Innovative Stitch Combinations

Unlock the door to creativity with innovative stitch combinations that add flair and uniqueness to your crochet projects. Let's explore the art of blending stitches to create stunning textures and patterns that elevate your amigurumi dolls to new heights.

1. Front and Back Post Stitches

Front and back post stitches create a ribbed effect, adding dimension and visual interest to your amigurumi. Technique:

- **Front Post Stitch:** Insert the hook from front to back around the post of the designated stitch, creating a raised ridge on the front side.
- **Back Post Stitch:** Insert the hook from back to front around the post of the designated stitch, pushing the post to the backside.

Tips: Experiment with alternating front and back post stitches to create intricate ribbing patterns. Use this technique for creating textured clothing or accessories for your amigurumi.

2. Bobble and Popcorn Stitches

Bobble and popcorn stitches add delightful 3D elements, perfect for creating unique features on your amigurumi dolls. Technique:

- **Bobble Stitch:** Work multiple incomplete double crochets in the same stitch, then yarn over and pull through all loops on the hook.
- **Popcorn Stitch:** Work multiple complete double crochets in the same stitch, then drop the loop, insert the hook in the first double crochet of the group, and pull the dropped loop through.

Tips: Strategically place bobbles for textured surfaces, like animal fur or flower centers. Use popcorn stitches to create playful, puffy embellishments.

3. Cable Stitch

Cable stitches mimic the appearance of knit cables, adding a touch of sophistication to your amigurumi. Technique:

- Cross stitches over each other by working stitches out of order.

Tips: Experiment with different crossing patterns to create intricate cable designs. It is ideal for crafting accessories like scarves or belts for your amigurumi.

4. Lace Stitch Patterns

Lace stitches introduce delicate and intricate patterns, perfect for adding a touch of elegance to your amigurumi. Technique:

- Create openwork patterns by combining chains, single crochets, and double crochets.

Tips: Use lace stitches to create ethereal garments or accessories for your dolls. It is ideal for crafting amigurumi with a fairy-tale theme.

5. Color Pooling
Color pooling involves manipulating variegated yarn to create planned patterns or designs. Technique:

- Pay attention to the color changes in your variegated yarn and strategically place stitches to create specific patterns.

Tips: Experiment with different stitch counts and yarn types to achieve desired color pooling effects. It is ideal for creating unique, personalized designs on your amigurumi.

Experimenting with innovative stitch combinations opens possibilities for your amigurumi creations. Let your imagination run wild as you blend these techniques to craft truly one-of-a-kind dolls.

6.4 Expert Tips for Efficiency

Efficiency in crochet not only saves time but also enhances the overall enjoyment of the crafting process. Let's delve into expert tips and techniques that will streamline your crocheting experience, making every stitch a joy.

1. Yarn Management
Efficient yarn management is the key to a smooth crocheting experience.

Tips: **Prevent Tangling:** Invest in yarn bowls or use homemade alternatives to keep your yarn from tangling as you work. **Use Yarn Holders:** For multi-color projects, use yarn holders or bobbins to keep your colors organized and prevent unnecessary tangling.

2. Hook Handling
How you handle your crochet hook can significantly impact your speed and comfort.

Tips: **Ergonomic Hooks:** Invest in ergonomic hooks that match your grip style. They reduce hand fatigue during extended crocheting sessions. **Proper Grip:** Hold your hook in a natural way that allows for swift movements. Experiment with pencil or knife grips to find what suits you best.

3. Project Planning
Efficiency starts with thoughtful project planning.

Tips: **Organize Supplies:** Before starting a project, gather all the necessary materials and organize them for easy access. **Plan Stitch Counts:** Plan your stitch counts for each row or round, reducing the need to frog (undo) your work due to mistakes.

4. Time Management

Making the most of your crafting time is essential, especially if you have a busy schedule.

Tips: **Set Realistic Goals:** Break your project into smaller, manageable goals to make it easier to track progress and prevent feeling overwhelmed. **Use Stitch Markers:** Strategically use stitch markers to identify critical points in your pattern, making it easier to keep track of your progress.

5. Pattern Familiarity

Thoroughly understanding your pattern contributes to a more efficient crochet session.

Tips: **Read Ahead:** Familiarize yourself with the pattern to anticipate stitches and transitions. **Highlight Key Instructions:** Use colored markers or digital highlighting tools to emphasize critical instructions in your pattern.

6. Tension Control

Maintaining consistent tension is crucial for a polished finished product.

Tips: **Practice Tension Techniques:** Regularly practice maintaining even tension with different stitch types to improve your overall crocheting experience. **Relax Your Grip:** A relaxed grip helps control tension. Be conscious of your hand muscles and avoid unnecessary tension.

7. Customize Your Workspace

Tailoring your workspace to your needs enhances efficiency.

Tips: **Good Lighting:** Ensure your workspace is well-lit to reduce eye strain and make it easier to see your stitches. **Comfortable Seating:** Invest in a comfortable chair and consider using cushions or pillows to support your back and neck.

Incorporating these expert tips into your crocheting routine will make the process more efficient and elevate the quality of your finished amigurumi dolls. Enjoy the journey of crafting with confidence and joy!

6.5 Exploring Unconventional Materials

Dare to venture beyond traditional yarn and explore the exciting realm of unconventional materials in crochet. Unleash your creativity as we delve into innovative options that can add unique textures, colors, and a touch of eco-consciousness to your amigurumi dolls.

1. Fabric Strips

Repurpose old fabric or use pre-cut strips to create vibrant, textured amigurumi projects.

Tips: **Cutting Techniques:** Learn various cutting techniques for different fabric types. Experiment with widths to achieve diverse textures. **Joining Fabric:** Explore methods like braiding or knotting to join fabric strips securely.

2. Plarn (Plastic Yarn)

Contribute to sustainability by transforming plastic bags into plarn for a durable and water-resistant crochet medium.

Tips: **Preparing Plarn:** Cut plastic bags into strips, join them, and roll them into a plarn ball. **Hook Selection:** Use a sturdy hook, as plastic can be more resistant than traditional yarn.

3. Paper Yarn

Infuse a touch of rustic charm into your amigurumi by incorporating paper yarn.

Tips: **Choosing Paper:** Explore different types of paper for varied textures. Consider handmade paper for an artisanal touch. **Coating Options:** To enhance durability, coat paper yarn projects with a sealant suitable for your chosen paper type.

4. Wires and Jewelry Findings

Introduce structure and possibility to your amigurumi by incorporating wires and jewelry findings.

Tips: **Wire Selection:** Choose pliable but sturdy wire. Test the wire's flexibility to ensure it holds the desired shape. **Securing Attachments:** Use jewelry findings like jump rings to attach limbs or accessories securely.

5. Burlap Twine

Embrace a rustic aesthetic by incorporating burlap twine for a textured and visually exciting outcome.

Tips: **Blending with Yarn:** Combine burlap twine with traditional yarn for a balanced texture. **Gauge Considerations:** Be mindful of the burlap's thickness; adjust your stitches accordingly.

6. Feathers and Faux Fur

Add a whimsical touch to your amigurumi by integrating feathers or faux fur for hair or embellishments.

Tips: **Attachment Techniques:** Secure feathers or faux fur by stitching them firmly into place. **Trimming and Shaping:** Trim feathers or faux fur to achieve desired lengths and shapes.

7. Natural Fibers

Explore fibers beyond the typical yarn spectrum, such as jute, hemp, or bamboo, for projects with a rustic or tropical vibe.

Tips: **Eco-Friendly Choices:** Opt for sustainably sourced natural fibers for an eco-conscious approach. **Blending Possibilities:** Combine natural fibers with traditional yarn to achieve unique textures.

Experimenting with unconventional materials opens up a world of possibilities in amigurumi design. As you embark on this creative journey, embrace the freedom to innovate and make each amigurumi doll a truly one-of-a-kind masterpiece.

6.6 Finishing Touches and Embellishments

Elevate your amigurumi creations to the next level by mastering the art of finishing touches and embellishments. These small details can transform a simple project into a personalized work of art, adding character, charm, and a touch of your unique style.

1. Embroidery Techniques

Enhance facial features and details with precise embroidery techniques.

Techniques:

- **Backstitch:** Create clean lines and outlines using the backstitch for eyes, mouths, and intricate designs.
- **French Knots:** Add texture and depth with French knots, perfect for creating small, raised embellishments.

2. Appliqué Additions

Introduce fabric appliqués for a playful and dynamic visual impact.

Tips: **Choosing Fabrics:** Opt for contrasting fabrics to make appliqués stand out. **Secure Stitching:** Attach appliqués securely to prevent fraying or loosening over time.

3. Bead and Button Embellishments

Tiny beads and buttons can bring sparkle and personality to your amigurumi dolls.

Techniques:

- **Sewing Beads:** Use tiny beads to create eyes, jewelry, or intricate patterns.

- **Button Joints:** Attach buttons to movable limbs' joints, adding function and flair.

4. Tassels and Pom-Poms

Incorporate playful tassels or pom-poms for a touch of whimsy.

Tips: **Yarn Selection:** Choose a contrasting or complementary yarn color for eye-catching tassels. **Uniformity:** Ensure consistency in size when creating multiple tassels or pom-poms.

5. Ribbon and Lace Accents

Delicate ribbon or lace can add a soft, elegant touch to your amigurumi.

Tips: **Attachment Methods:** Stitch or glue ribbon and lace carefully to avoid damage to the material. **Layering Possibilities:** Experiment with different layering and ribbons for a unique effect.

6. Painted Details

Unleash your artistic side by incorporating painted details.

Techniques:

- **Fabric Paints:** Use fabric-safe paints to add intricate details or patterns.
- **Sealing Finishes:** Apply a fabric sealant to ensure longevity and prevent fading.

7. Fringe and Hair Details

Create distinctive hairstyles or textured surfaces using fringe or yarn loops.

Tips: **Precision Cutting:** Cut fringe evenly for a polished look. **Secure Attachment:** securely stitch fringe to prevent unraveling.

8. Cord and Belt Embellishments

Integrate small cords or belts for additional character and definition.

Tips: **Creating Belts:** Crochet or sew miniature belts to enhance the waistline. **Cord as Accessories:** Use thin cords to craft accessories like belts, bracelets, or necklaces.

Mastering the art of finishing touches and embellishments is the final step in creating amigurumi dolls that reflect your creativity and attention to detail. Experiment with different techniques, mix, and match embellishments, and let your imagination run wild to make each amigurumi uniquely yours.

Chapter 7: Classic Doll Pattern

7.1 Ballerina Doll

Materials Needed:

- Worsted weight yarn in skin tone, tutu color, and hair color
- Crochet hook appropriate for your yarn weight
- Safety eyes
- Stuffing material
- Yarn needle
- Stitch markers
- Black embroidery thread or yarn for mouth
- Pink felt for ballet slippers
- Fabric glue
- Scissors

Note:

Work in continuous rounds, do not join at the end of each round. Use a stitch marker to keep track of the beginning of each round.

1. **Head:**
- Row 1: Magic ring, 6 sc in ring. (6)
- Row 2: Inc around. (12)
- Row 3: Sc 1, inc around. (18)
- Row 4: Sc 2, inc around. (24)
- Row 5: Sc 3, inc around. (30)
- Row 6-10: Sc around. (30)
- Row 11: Sc 3, dec around. (24)
- Row 12: Sc 2, dec around. (18)
- Row 13: Sc 1, dec around. (12)
- Row 14: Dec around. (6)

Finish off, leaving a long tail for sewing. Stuff the head.

2. **Body:**
- Row 1: Magic ring, 6 sc in ring. (6)

- Row 2: Inc around. (12)
- Row 3: Sc 1, inc around. (18)
- Rows 4-8. Sc around. (18)

Finish off, leaving a long tail for sewing. Stuff the body.

3. Arms (make 2):

- Magic ring, 5 sc in ring. (5)
- 2-7. Sc around. (5)

Finish off, leaving a long tail for sewing.

4. Legs (make 2):

- Magic ring, 6 sc in ring. (6)
- 2-3. Sc around. (6)

Finish off, leaving a long tail for sewing. Do not stuff the legs.

5. Tutu:

Row 1:

- Make a slip knot and chain a multiple of 6 stitches. This will determine the width of your tutu. For example, you can chain 30 for a standard-sized doll tutu. Join the chain into a ring with a slip stich.
- Join the chain into a ring with a slip stich.

Row 2:

- Turn your work. Skip the first chain.
- Work 1 dc in the next stitch.
- Ch 2, then work 1 dc in the same stitch.
- Skip 2 stitches, then work (1 dc, ch 2, 1 dc) in the next stitch. Repeat from * to * across the row.
- End with a slip stitch in the first dc.

Row 3:

- Turn your work. Slip stitch into the first ch-2 space.
- Ch 3 (this counts as your first dc), then work 2 dc, ch 2, 3 dc into the same ch-2 space.
- In the next ch-2 space, work (3 dc, ch 2, 3 dc). Repeat from * to * across the row.
- End with a slip stitch in the top of the turning chain.

Row 4:

- Turn your work. Slip stitch into the next 3 dc and ch-2 space.
- Ch 3 (this counts as your first dc), then work 2 dc, ch 2, 3 dc into the same ch-2 space.
- In the next ch-2 space, work (3 dc, ch 2, 3 dc). Repeat from * to * across the row.
- End with a slip stitch in the top of the turning chain.

Fasten off and weave in any loose ends. Attach the tutu to your doll by sewing it securely around the doll's waist. This pattern creates a lovely and full tutu for your ballerina doll. Adjust the number of chains in Row 1 for a wider or narrower tutu, depending on your preference. Remember to customize the colors to match your doll's outfit and style.

Hair:

Attach hair color yarn to the top of the head and crochet chains to desired hair length. Trim and style as desired.

Assembly:

Attach safety eyes to the head, positioning them between rounds 7 and 8, leaving a few stitches between them.

Embroider a small mouth below the eyes using black embroidery thread or yarn.

Attach the arms to the sides of the body.

Attach the head to the body.

Attach the legs to the bottom of the body.

Cut small ovals from pink felt and glue them to the bottom of the legs for ballet slippers.

Your ballerina doll is complete! You can customize the colors and details to create your own unique ballet dancer. Happy crocheting!

7.2 Victorian Doll

Materials Needed:

- Worsted weight yarn in skin tone, dress color, bonnet color, and hair color
- Crochet hook appropriate for your yarn weight
- Safety eyes
- Stuffing material
- Yarn needle
- Stitch markers
- Black embroidery thread or yarn for mouth

- Lace or ribbon for dress and bonnet
- Scissors
- Ribbon for ties (optional)

Note:

Work in continuous rounds, do not join at the end of each round. Use a stitch marker to keep track of the beginning of each round.

1. **Head:**
- Magic ring, 6 sc in ring. (6)
- Inc around. (12)
- Sc 1, inc around. (18)
- Sc 2, inc around. (24)
- Sc 3, inc around. (30)
- 6-10. Sc around. (30)
- Sc 3, dec around. (24)
- Sc 2, dec around. (18)
- Sc 1, dec around. (12)
- Dec around. (6)

Finish off, leaving a long tail for sewing. Stuff the head.

2. **Body:**
- Magic ring, 6 sc in ring. (6)
- Inc around. (12)
- Sc 1, inc around. (18)
- 4-9. Sc around. (18)

Finish off, leaving a long tail for sewing. Stuff the body.

3. **Arms (make 2):**
- Magic ring, 5 sc in ring. (5)
- 2-5. Sc around. (5)

Finish off, leaving a long tail for sewing.

4. **Legs (make 2):**
- Magic ring, 6 sc in ring. (6)
- 2-3. Sc around. (6)

Finish off, leaving a long tail for sewing. Do not stuff the legs.

5. **Dress:**

Row 1 (Bodice):

- Make a slip knot and chain a multiple of 8 stitches plus 1. This will determine the width of the bodice. For example, you can chain 25 for a standard-sized doll bodice.
- Turn your work. Skip the first chain from the hook, then work 1 sc in each chain across. (24)

Row 2 (Bodice):

- Ch 1 (counts as first sc), turn your work.
- Work 1 sc in each of the next 5 stitches.
- Ch 2, skip 2 stitches, work 1 sc in each of the next 4 stitches. Repeat from * to * twice more.
- Ch 2, skip 2 stitches, work 1 sc in each of the last 5 stitches.

Row 3 (Bodice):

- Ch 1, turn your work.
- Work 1 sc in each of the first 5 stitches.
- 2 sc in the ch-2 space, 1 sc in each of the next 4 stitches. Repeat from * to * twice more.
- 2 sc in the ch-2 space, 1 sc in each of the last 5 stitches. (24)

Rows 4-6 (Bodice):

- Repeat Rows 2 and 3, then Row 2 once more. (24)

Row 7 (Sleeves):

- Ch 1, turn your work.
- Work 1 sc in each of the first 4 stitches.
- Ch 7, skip 4 stitches, then work 1 sc in each of the next 8 stitches.
- Ch 7, skip 4 stitches, then work 1 sc in each of the last 4 stitches.

Rows 8 (Sleeves):

- Ch 1, turn your work.
- Work 1 sc in each stitch and 7 sc in each chain space.

Rows 9 (Sleeves):

- Ch 1, turn your work.
- Work 1 sc in each stitch across the row.

Skirt:

Row 1:

- Change to a new color for the skirt.
- Ch 2 (counts as first hdc), turn your work.
- Work 1 hdc in each stitch across the row.

Rows 2-8:

- Ch 2 (counts as first hdc), turn your work.
- Work 1 hdc in each stitch across the row.

Finishing:

- Fasten off and weave in any loose ends.
- Fold the bodice in half and sew the side seams.
- Attach buttons or other embellishments as desired.

This pattern creates a beautiful Victorian-style dress for your doll. Customize the colors and embellishments to suit your doll's style. Enjoy creating your Victorian doll's dress!

6. Bonnet:

Using bonnet color yarn, create a small circle for the top of the bonnet. Then, create a rectangle for the brim of the bonnet. Attach lace or ribbon for embellishment.

Brim:

Row 1:

- Make a slip knot and chain 9.
- Turn your work. Skip the first chain from the hook, then work 1 sc in each of the next 8 chains. (8)

Rows 2-6:

- Ch 1 (counts as first sc), turn your work.
- Work 1 sc in each stitch across. (8)

Row 7:

- Ch 1, turn your work.
- Work 2 sc in the first stitch.
- 1 sc in each of the next 6 stitches, 2 sc in the last stitch. Repeat from * to * once more. (10)

Row 8:

- Ch 1, turn your work.

- Work 1 sc in each stitch across. (10)

Row 9:

- Ch 1, turn your work.
- Work 2 sc in the first stitch.
- 1 sc in each of the next 8 stitches, 2 sc in the last stitch. Repeat from * to * once more. (12)

Row 10:

- Ch 1, turn your work.
- Work 1 sc in each stitch across. (12)

Row 11:

- Ch 1, turn your work.
- Work 2 sc in the first stitch.
- 1 sc in each of the next 10 stitches, 2 sc in the last stitch. Repeat from * to * once more. (14)

Row 12:

- Ch 1, turn your work.
- Work 1 sc in each stitch across. (14)

Fasten off and leave a long tail for sewing.

Bonnet Body:

Fold the brim in half lengthwise, lining up the edges. Using the long tail and a yarn needle, sew the two edges together.

Ruffles:

- Attach the yarn on one side of the brim (where you started the chain).
- Ch 1, then work 1 sc in the same stitch. Work 2 sc in each stitch around the brim.
- Join with a slip stitch to the first sc.

Fasten off and weave in any loose ends.

Ties (optional):

- Cut two pieces of ribbon, each about 12 inches long.
- Attach one end of each ribbon to the corners of the bonnet.

Your Victorian doll now has a charming bonnet to complete her ensemble! Adjust the size as needed to fit your specific doll.

Assembly:

- Attach safety eyes to the head, positioning them between rounds 7 and 8, leaving a few stitches between them.
- Embroider a small mouth below the eyes using black embroidery thread or yarn.
- Attach the arms to the sides of the body.
- Attach the head to the body.
- Attach the legs to the bottom of the body.
- Attach the dress around the body, ensuring the openings for the arms align.
- Attach the bonnet to the head, positioning it over the hair.

Your Victorian Doll is complete! You can customize the colors and details to create your own elegant doll reminiscent of the Victorian era. Happy crocheting!

7.3 Retro Pin Up Doll

Materials Needed:

- Worsted weight yarn in skin tone, dress color, headscarf color, and hair color
- Crochet hook appropriate for your yarn weight
- Safety eyes
- Stuffing material
- Yarn needle
- Stitch markers
- Black embroidery thread or yarn for mouth
- Small amount of white yarn for polka dots (optional)
- Scissors

Note:

Work in continuous rounds, do not join at the end of each round. Use a stitch marker to keep track of the beginning of each round.

1. **Head:**
- Magic ring, 6 sc in ring. (6)
- Inc around. (12)
- Sc 1, inc around. (18)
- Sc 2, inc around. (24)
- Sc 3, inc around. (30)

- 6-10. Sc around. (30)
- Sc 3, dec around. (24)
- Sc 2, dec around. (18)
- Sc 1, dec around. (12)
- Dec around. (6)

Finish off, leaving a long tail for sewing. Stuff the head.

2. Body:
- Magic ring, 6 sc in ring. (6)
- Inc around. (12)
- Sc 1, inc around. (18)
- 4-9. Sc around. (18)

Finish off, leaving a long tail for sewing. Stuff the body.

3. Arms (make 2):
- Magic ring, 5 sc in ring. (5)
- 2-6. Sc around. (5)

Finish off, leaving a long tail for sewing.

4. Legs (make 2):
- Magic ring, 6 sc in ring. (6)
- 2-4. Sc around. (6)

Finish off, leaving a long tail for sewing. Do not stuff the legs.

5. Dress:

Using dress color yarn, create a rectangle that fits around the doll's body. Leave openings for the arms. Optionally, add white yarn for polka dots. Add a row of contrasting color for the hem of the dress.

Bodice:

Row 1:
- Make a slip knot and chain a multiple of 6 stitches plus 1. This will determine the width of the bodice. For example, you can chain 25 for a standard-sized doll bodice.
- Turn your work. Skip the first chain from the hook, then work 1 sc in each chain across. (24)

Row 2:

- Ch 1 (counts as first sc), turn your work.
- Work 1 sc in each of the next 5 stitches.
- Ch 2, skip 2 stitches, work 1 sc in each of the next 4 stitches. Repeat from * to * twice more.
- Ch 2, skip 2 stitches, work 1 sc in each of the last 5 stitches.

Row 3:

- Ch 1, turn your work.
- Work 1 sc in each of the first 5 stitches.
- 2 sc in the ch-2 space, 1 sc in each of the next 4 stitches. Repeat from * to * twice more.
- 2 sc in the ch-2 space, 1 sc in each of the last 5 stitches. (24)

Rows 4-6:

- Repeat Rows 2 and 3, then Row 2 once more. (24)

Skirt:

Row 1:

- Change to a new color for the skirt.
- Ch 2 (counts as first hdc), turn your work.
- Work 1 hdc in each stitch across the row.

Rows 2-10:

- Ch 2 (counts as first hdc), turn your work.
- Work 1 hdc in each stitch across the row.

Fasten off and weave in any loose ends. Attach buttons or other embellishments as desired.

This pattern creates a lovely retro-inspired dress for your pin-up doll. Customize the colors and embellishments to suit your doll's style.

6. Headscarf:

Using headscarf color yarn, create a long strip. Tie it around the doll's head and secure in place.

Foundation:

- Make a slip knot and chain 11.
- Row 1: Turn your work. Skip the first chain from the hook, then work 1 sc in each of the next 10 chains. (10)
- Row 2: Ch 1 (counts as first sc), turn your work. Work 1 sc in each of the next 10 stitches.

- Row 3: Ch 3 (counts as first dc), turn your work. Work 1 dc in each of the next 10 stitches.
- Row 4: Ch 1 (counts as first sc), turn your work. Work 1 sc in each of the next 10 stitches.
- Rows 5-24: Repeat Rows 3 and 4 until you have a total of 24 rows. Adjust the number of rows if you'd like a longer or shorter headscarf.

Edging:
- Ch 1, turn your work.
- Work 1 sc in each of the next 10 stitches.
- Work 3 sc in the last stitch (corner).
- Rotate your work to crochet along the edge of the headscarf. Work 1 sc in each row-end stitch.

Fasten off and weave in any loose ends.

Ties:
- Attach yarn to one corner of the headscarf.
- Ch 35 (adjust as needed for desired tie length).

Fasten off and repeat on the other corner of the headscarf.

Assembly:
- Attach safety eyes to the head, positioning them between rounds 7 and 8, leaving a few stitches between them.
- Embroider a small mouth below the eyes using black embroidery thread or yarn.
- Attach the arms to the sides of the body.
- Attach the head to the body.
- Attach the legs to the bottom of the body.
- Attach the dress around the body, ensuring the openings for the arms align.
- Tie the headscarf around the doll's head, positioning it as desired.

Your Retro Pin-Up Doll is complete! You can customize the colors and details to create your own 1950s-inspired doll. Happy crocheting!

7.4 Japanese Kokeshi Doll

Materials Needed:
- Worsted weight yarn in doll body color, kimono color, hair color, and floral pattern color

- Crochet hook appropriate for your yarn weight
- Safety eyes
- Stuffing material
- Yarn needle
- Stitch markers
- Black embroidery thread or yarn for mouth
- Small felt circles for cheeks (optional)

Note:

Work in continuous rounds, do not join at the end of each round. Use a stitch marker to keep track of the beginning of each round.

1. **Head:**
- Magic ring, 6 sc in ring. (6)
- Inc around. (12)
- Sc 1, inc around. (18)
- Sc 2, inc around. (24)
- Sc 3, inc around. (30)
- 6-10. Sc around. (30)
- Sc 3, dec around. (24)
- Sc 2, dec around. (18)
- Sc 1, dec around. (12)
- Dec around. (6)

Finish off, leaving a long tail for sewing. Stuff the head.

2. **Body:**
- Magic ring, 6 sc in ring. (6)
- Inc around. (12)
- Sc 1, inc around. (18)
- 4-9. Sc around. (18)

Finish off, leaving a long tail for sewing. Stuff the body.

3. **Arms (make 2):**
- Magic ring, 5 sc in ring. (5)
- 2-6. Sc around. (5)

Finish off, leaving a long tail for sewing.

4. Legs (make 2):
- Magic ring, 6 sc in ring. (6)
- 2-4. Sc around. (6)

Finish off, leaving a long tail for sewing. Do not stuff the legs.

5. Kimono:

Using kimono color yarn, create a rectangle that fits around the doll's body. Leave openings for the arms. Optionally, add contrasting color for sleeves and an obi belt.

Back Panel:

Row 1:
- Make a slip knot and chain a multiple of 6 stitches plus 1. This will determine the width of the back panel. For example, you can chain 19 for a standard-sized doll back panel.
- Turn your work. Skip the first chain from the hook, then work 1 sc in each chain across. (18)

Rows 2-20:
- Ch 1 (counts as first sc), turn your work.
- Work 1 sc in each stitch across. (18)

Front Panels (Make 2):

Row 1:
- Make a slip knot and chain a multiple of 6 stitches plus 1. This will determine the width of each front panel. For example, you can chain 13 for a standard-sized doll front panel.
- Turn your work. Skip the first chain from the hook, then work 1 sc in each chain across. (12)

Rows 2-20:
- Ch 1 (counts as first sc), turn your work.
- Work 1 sc in each stitch across. (12)

Sleeves (Make 2):

Row 1:
- Make a slip knot and chain 10.

- Turn your work. Skip the first chain from the hook, then work 1 sc in each of the next 9 chains. (9)

Rows 2-8:

- Ch 1 (counts as first sc), turn your work.
- Work 1 sc in each stitch across. (9)

Assembly:

Lay the back panel flat. Attach one front panel to each side by slip stitching along the top edge. Attach the sleeves by slip stitching them to the sides of the front and back panels.

Belt:

- Attach yarn at the waistline of the kimono.
- Ch 60 (adjust as needed for desired belt length).

Fasten off and weave in any loose ends. Customize the colors and embellishments to suit style.

Hair:

Attach hair color yarn to the top of the head and crochet chains to desired hair length. Trim and style as desired.

Floral Pattern:

Using floral pattern color yarn, create simple flower motifs to sew onto the kimono.

Assembly:

- Attach safety eyes to the head, positioning them between rounds 7 and 8, leaving a few stitches between them.
- Embroider a small mouth below the eyes using black embroidery thread or yarn. Optionally, glue small felt circles for cheeks.
- Attach the arms to the sides of the body.
- Attach the head to the body.
- Attach the legs to the bottom of the body.
- Attach the kimono around the body, ensuring the openings for the arms align.
- Sew on the floral patterns as desired.

Your Japanese Kokeshi Doll is complete! You can customize the colors and details to create your own collection of elegant traditional dolls. Happy crocheting!

Chapter 8: Modern Doll Pattern

8.1 Fashionista Doll

Materials Needed:
- Worsted weight yarn in skin tone, blue yarn for the jacket, complementary color for the skirt, color of your choice for the handbag
- Crochet hook appropriate for your yarn weight
- Yarn needle for sewing and weaving in ends
- Safety eyes
- Stuffing material
- Stitch markers
- Black embroidery thread or yarn for mouth
- Small buttons, beads, or charms for accessories

Note:

Work in continuous rounds, do not join at the end of each round. Use a stitch marker to keep track of the beginning of each round.

1. **Head:**
- Magic ring, 6 sc in ring. (6)
- Inc around. (12)
- Sc 1, inc around. (18)
- Sc 2, inc around. (24)
- Sc 3, inc around. (30) 6-10. Sc around. (30)
- Sc 3, dec around. (24)
- Sc 2, dec around. (18)
- Sc 1, dec around. (12)
- Dec around. (6)

Finish off, leaving a long tail for sewing. Stuff the head.

2. **Body:**
- Magic ring, 6 sc in ring. (6)
- Inc around. (12)
- Sc 1, inc around. (18) 4-9. Sc around. (18)

Finish off, leaving a long tail for sewing. Stuff the body.

3. Arms (make 2):

- Magic ring, 5 sc in ring. (5)
- 2-7. Sc around. (5)

Finish off, leaving a long tail for sewing.

4. Legs (make 2):

- Magic ring, 6 sc in ring. (6)
- 2-6. Sc around. (6)

Finish off, leaving a long tail for sewing. Do not stuff the legs.

5. Denim Jacket:

Jacket Back:

- Start with a Magic Ring.
- Round 1: Ch 1, 6 sc into the Magic Ring. (6)
- Rounds 2-8: Sc in each stitch around. (6)
- Fasten off.

Jacket Front:

- Start with a Magic Ring.
- Round 1: Ch 1, 5 sc into the Magic Ring. (5)
- Rounds 2-8: Sc in each stitch around. (5)
- Fasten off.

Sleeves (Make 2):

- Start with a Magic Ring.
- Round 1: Ch 1, 6 sc into the Magic Ring. (6)
- Rounds 2-6: Sc in each stitch around. (6)
- Fasten off.
- Assembly:

Attach the jacket fronts to the jacket back, leaving openings for the arms. Attach the sleeves to the armholes. Add buttons or decorative elements if desired.

6. Trendy Handbag:

Base of the Handbag:

- Start with a Magic Ring.
- Round 1: Ch 1, 6 sc into the Magic Ring. (6)
- Round 2: Inc in each stitch around. (12)
- Round 3: Sc, Inc around. (18)
- Round 4: Sc in the next 2 sts, Inc around. (24)
- Round 5: Sc in the next 3 sts, Inc around. (30)
- Round 6: Sc in the next 4 sts, Inc around. (36)
- Round 7: Sc in the next 5 sts, Inc around. (42)
- Rounds 8-12: Sc in each stitch around. (42)
- Fasten off.

Flap:

- Attach yarn at one end of the base.
- Row 1: Ch 1, sc in the same st and in the next 20 sts. Turn. (21)
- Rows 2-8: Ch 1, sc in each st across. Turn. (21)
- Fasten off.

Strap:

- Attach yarn at one side of the handbag.
- Row 1: Ch 1, sc in the same st and in the next 10 sts. Turn. (11)
- Rows 2-60 (adjust length if desired): Ch 1, sc in each st across. Turn. (11)
- Fasten off.

Assembly:

Fold the flap down over the front of the handbag. Sew the sides of the flap to the sides of the handbag to create a closure. Attach the strap to the sides of the handbag, positioning it to your desired length. Weave in all ends.

Your Fashionista Doll is complete! You can customize the colors and details to create your own trendy doll with a fashionable wardrobe. Happy crocheting!

8.2 Traveler Doll

Materials Needed:

- Worsted weight yarn in skin tone, color of your choice for the pants, for the shirt, for the backpack, and travel accessories
- Crochet hook appropriate for your yarn weight
- Safety eyes
- Stuffing material
- Yarn needle
- Stitch markers
- Black embroidery thread or yarn for mouth
- Small buttons or charms for accessories

Note:

Work in continuous rounds, do not join at the end of each round. Use a stitch marker to keep track of the beginning of each round.

1. **Head:**
- Magic ring, 6 sc in ring. (6)
- Inc around. (12)
- Sc 1, inc around. (18)
- Sc 2, inc around. (24)
- Sc 3, inc around. (30)
- 6-10. Sc around. (30)
- Sc 3, dec around. (24)
- Sc 2, dec around. (18)
- Sc 1, dec around. (12)
- Dec around. (6)

Finish off, leaving a long tail for sewing. Stuff the head.

2. **Body:**
- Magic ring, 6 sc in ring. (6)
- Inc around. (12)
- Sc 1, inc around. (18)
- 4-9. Sc around. (18)

Finish off, leaving a long tail for sewing. Stuff the body.

3. **Arms (make 2):**

- Magic ring, 5 sc in ring. (5)
- 2-7. Sc around. (5)

Finish off, leaving a long tail for sewing.

4. Legs (make 2):
- Magic ring, 6 sc in ring. (6)
- 2-6. Sc around. (6)

Finish off, leaving a long tail for sewing. Do not stuff the legs.

5. Cargo Pants:

Legs (Make 2):
- Start with a Magic Ring.
- Round 1: Ch 1, 6 sc into the Magic Ring. (6)
- Rounds 2-6: Sc in each stitch around. (6)
- Fasten off.

Upper Part of Pants:
- Attach yarn to one of the legs.
- Row 1: Ch 1, sc in the same st and in the next 5 sts. Turn. (6)
- Rows 2-8: Ch 1, sc in each st across. Turn. (6)
- Fasten off.
- Attach yarn to the other leg and repeat rows 1-4.

Assembly:
- Fold the upper part of the pants in half, matching up the legs.
- Sew the sides of the legs and the crotch area using whipstitch or your preferred seaming method.
- Weave in all ends.

6. Traveler's Shirt:

Front Panel:
- Start with a Magic Ring.
- Round 1: Ch 1, 6 sc into the Magic Ring. (6)
- Rounds 2-4: Sc in each stitch around. (6)
- Fasten off.

Back Panel:

- Start with a Magic Ring.
- Round 1: Ch 1, 6 sc into the Magic Ring. (6)
- Rounds 2-4: Sc in each stitch around. (6)
- Fasten off.

Sleeves (Make 2):

- Start with a Magic Ring.
- Round 1: Ch 1, 6 sc into the Magic Ring. (6)
- Rounds 2-3: Sc in each stitch around. (6)
- Fasten off.

Assembly:

- Attach the front and back panels together at the sides using whipstitch or your preferred seaming method.
- Attach the sleeves to the armholes.
- Weave in all ends.

Accessories:

1. **Backpack**: Crochet a rectangle, fold it in half, and attach straps. Add a button or drawstring closure.Attach it to the doll's back.
2. **Camera**: Create a rectangular shape for the body and attach a circular piece for the lens.
3. **Map**: Crochet a small rectangle and add details with embroidery thread.

Assembly:

- Attach safety eyes to the head, positioning them between rounds 7 and 8, leaving a few stitches between them.
- Embroider a small mouth below the eyes using black embroidery thread or yarn.
- Attach the arms to the sides of the body.
- Attach the head to the body.
- Attach the legs to the bottom of the body.
- Dress the doll in the chosen outfit and accessorize with the backpack, camera, and other travel essentials.

Your Traveler Doll is complete! You can customize the colors and details to create your own adventurous explorer. Happy crocheting!

8.3 Fitness Enthusiast Doll

Materials Needed:

- Worsted weight yarn in skin tone, workout attire colors for the body, for the sneakers, yoga mat color, dumbbell colors, and fitness accessory colors
- Crochet hook appropriate for your yarn weight
- Safety eyes
- Stuffing material
- Yarn needle
- Stitch markers
- Small beads for dumbbells (optional)

Note:

Work in continuous rounds, do not join at the end of each round. Use a stitch marker to keep track of the beginning of each round.

1. **Head:**

- Magic ring, 6 sc in ring. (6)
- Inc around. (12)
- Sc 1, inc around. (18)
- Sc 2, inc around. (24)
- Sc 3, inc around. (30)
- 6-10. Sc around. (30)
- Sc 3, dec around. (24)
- Sc 2, dec around. (18)
- Sc 1, dec around. (12)
- Dec around. (6)

Finish off, leaving a long tail for sewing. Stuff the head.

2. **Body:**

- Magic ring, 6 sc in ring. (6)
- Inc around. (12)
- Sc 1, inc around. (18)

- 4-9. Sc around. (18)

Finish off, leaving a long tail for sewing. Stuff the body.

3. **Arms (make 2):**
- Magic ring, 5 sc in ring. (5)
- 2-7. Sc around. (5)

Finish off, leaving a long tail for sewing.

4. **Legs (make 2):**
- Magic ring, 6 sc in ring. (6)
- 2-6. Sc around. (6)

Finish off, leaving a long tail for sewing. Do not stuff the legs.

5. **Workout Attire - Fitness Body:**
- Start at the top of the body.
- Ch 9.
- Row 1: Sc in the 2nd ch from hook and in each ch across. Turn. (8)
- Rows 2-12: Ch 1, sc in each st across. Turn. (8)
- Row 13: Ch 1, sc in the first 4 sts, ch 2 (this creates the armhole), sc in the last 4 sts. Turn. (8)
- Rows 14-17: Ch 1, sc in each st and ch across. Turn. (8)
- Row 18: Ch 1, sc in the first 4 sts, 2 sc in the ch-2 space, sc in the last 4 sts. Turn. (10)
- Rows 19-25: Ch 1, sc in each st across. Turn. (10)
- Fasten off.

Assembly:
- Fold the body in half along the row with the armholes.
- Seam the sides and underarm area using whipstitch or your preferred seaming method.
- Weave in all ends.

6. **Sneakers:**

Shoe Sole (Make 2):
- Ch 6.
- Row 1: Sc in the 2nd ch from hook, sc in next 3 ch, 3 sc in the last ch. Working on the other side of the chain, sc in next 3 ch, 2 sc in the last ch. Join with a sl st to the first sc. (12)

- Fasten off.

Shoe Upper (Make 2):
- Attach yarn to any stitch on the shoe sole.
- Round 1: Ch 1, sc in the same st and in the next 10 sts. (11)
- Rounds 2-4: Sc in each stitch around. (11)
- Fasten off.

Assembly:

Attach the shoe upper to the shoe sole using whipstitch or your preferred seaming method. Weave in all ends.

Laces (Optional):

Cut a small piece of contrasting yarn and thread it through the holes in the shoe upper to create laces.

Fitness Accessories:
- *Headband:* Ch 40. Fasten off.
- *Dumbbells (Make 2):* Ch 6. Round 1: Sc in the 2nd ch from hook and in each ch around. Join with a sl st to the first sc. (5). Fasten off.
- *Yoga Mat:* Using yoga mat color yarn, create a rectangular piece to resemble a yoga mat. Optionally, add a strap for easy carrying.

Assembly:
- Attach safety eyes to the head, positioning them between rounds 7 and 8, leaving a few stitches between them.
- Embroider a small mouth below the eyes using black embroidery thread or yarn.
- Attach the arms to the sides of the body.
- Attach the head to the body.
- Attach the legs to the bottom of the body.

Your Fitness Enthusiast Doll is complete! You can customize the colors and details to create your own health-conscious doll. Happy crocheting!

8.4 Foodie Doll

Materials Needed:

- Worsted weight yarn in skin tone, color of your choice for the jacket, the pants, food item colors, chef hat color, and kitchen utensil colors
- Crochet hook appropriate for your yarn weight
- Safety eyes
- Stuffing material
- Yarn needle
- Stitch markers
- Small buttons or beads for food details (optional)

Note:

Work in continuous rounds, do not join at the end of each round. Use a stitch marker to keep track of the beginning of each round.

1. **Head:**
- Magic ring, 6 sc in ring. (6)
- Inc around. (12)
- Sc 1, inc around. (18)
- Sc 2, inc around. (24)
- Sc 3, inc around. (30) 6-10. Sc around. (30)
- Sc 3, dec around. (24)
- Sc 2, dec around. (18)
- Sc 1, dec around. (12)
- Dec around. (6) Finish off, leaving a long tail for sewing. Stuff the head.

2. **Body:**
- Magic ring, 6 sc in ring. (6)
- Inc around. (12)
- Sc 1, inc around. (18) 4-9. Sc around. (18) Finish off, leaving a long tail for sewing. Stuff the body.

3. **Arms (make 2):**
- Magic ring, 5 sc in ring. (5)
- 2-7. Sc around. (5)
- Finish off, leaving a long tail for sewing.

4. **Legs (make 2):**

- Magic ring, 6 sc in ring. (6)
- 2-6. Sc around. (6)
- Finish off, leaving a long tail for sewing. Do not stuff the legs.

Assembly:
- Attach safety eyes to the head, positioning them between rounds 7 and 8, leaving a few stitches between them.
- Embroider a small mouth below the eyes using black embroidery thread or yarn.
- Attach the arms to the sides of the body.
- Attach the head to the body.
- Attach the legs to the bottom of the body.

5. Chef's Jacket:

Front Panels (Make 2):
- Ch 13.
- Row 1: Sc in the 2nd ch from hook and in each ch across. Turn. (12)
- Rows 2-6: Ch 1, sc in each st across. Turn. (12)
- Fasten off.

Back Panel:
- Ch 24.
- Row 1: Sc in the 2nd ch from hook and in each ch across. Turn. (23)
- Rows 2-6: Ch 1, sc in each st across. Turn. (23)
- Fasten off.

Assembly:
- Attach the front panels to the sides of the back panel using whipstitch or your preferred seaming method.
- Seam the sides and shoulders.
- Weave in all ends.

6. Chef's Pants:

Legs (Make 2):
- Ch 7.
- Row 1: Sc in the 2nd ch from hook and in each ch across. Turn. (6)
- Rows 2-13: Ch 1, sc in each st across. Turn. (6)

- Fasten off.

Assembly:
- Fold each leg in half, matching up the edges.
- Seam the sides of the legs.
- Attach the pants to the doll.
- Weave in all ends.

7. Chef's Hat:
- Start with a Magic Ring.
- Round 1: Ch 1, 6 sc into the Magic Ring. (6)
- Round 2: Sc in each st around. (6)
- Rounds 3-5: Ch 1, sc in each st around. (6)
- Round 6: [Sc, inc] around. (9)
- Rounds 7-10: Ch 1, sc in each st around. (9)
- Round 11: [Sc, inc] around. (13)
- Rounds 12-15: Ch 1, sc in each st around. (13)
- Fasten off, leaving a long tail for sewing.

Assembly:
- Thread the yarn tail through a yarn needle.
- Gather the opening of the hat and pull it closed.
- Secure the yarn tightly and weave in the end.
- Attach the hat to the doll's head.

Food Items anf Kitchen Utensils ideas:
1. **Chef's Knife.** Materials: Grey or silver yarn for the blade, black yarn for the handle. Pattern: Crochet a blade shape and a handle separately, then attach them together.
2. **Spatula**. Materials: Brown or black yarn for the handle, a lighter color for the spatula part. Pattern: Create a handle shape and a flat, wide spatula part separately, then attach them together.
3. **Whisk**. Materials: Grey or silver yarn for the wire loops, a contrasting color for the handle. Pattern: Crochet the loops and handle separately, then attach them together.
4. **Rolling Pin.** Materials: Brown or tan yarn for the pin, a contrasting color for the handles. Pattern: Create a cylindrical shape for the pin and two handle shapes, then

attach them together.

5. **Mixing Bowl and Spoon**. Materials: Yarn in a color of your choice for the bowl, a contrasting color for the spoon. Pattern: Crochet a bowl shape and a spoon separately, then place the spoon inside the bowl.

6. **Measuring Cups and Spoons**. Materials: Different colors of yarn for each cup or spoon. Pattern: Create cylindrical shapes for the cups and spoon parts, then add handles.

7. **Pot with Lid**. Materials: Yarn in a color of your choice for the pot, a contrasting color for the lid. Pattern: Crochet a cylindrical shape for the pot and a flat circle for the lid, then attach them.

Your Foodie Doll is complete! You can customize the colors and details to create your own culinary enthusiast doll. Remember to adjust the size of the utensils to fit your Amigurumi Doll appropriately. You can also add details like handles, markings, or knobs to make them more realistic. Enjoy crafting!

Conclusion: Embracing the Creative Journey

Dear Readers,

As we reach the end of this creative journey into the enchanting world of amigurumi, I genuinely want to express my gratitude to each of you for joining me on this colorful and imaginative adventure. Your creativity is a unique thread that weaves through every stitch and embellishment, bringing life and personality to your amigurumi dolls. The beauty of this craft lies not only in the final creations but also in the individuality each of you imparts to your projects.

I encourage you to find inspiration in the world around you. Nature, art, stories, and everyday moments can spark ideas that transform into the next whimsical creation. Keep your eyes open to the beauty surrounding you and let your imagination free.

Remember, each stitch tells a story, and every embellishment expresses your unique style. Don't hesitate to infuse your personality into the patterns, making them your own. Let your creativity flow, whether it's a subtle change in color, a personalized accessory, or an entirely original design. Connect with fellow crocheters, share your experiences, and celebrate the joy of creating together. Our exploration of amigurumi is just the beginning. Continue to seek new patterns, experiment with different techniques, and embrace the joy that comes with each completed project. The beauty of crochet lies in its endless possibilities, and there's always something new to discover and create. I invite you to see every yarn strand as an endless thread of possibility. As you crochet, you're not just crafting dolls but weaving stories, memories, and moments of joy. Embrace the creative journey, relish in the process, and let your imagination soar.

Thank you for being part of this beautiful expedition into amigurumi. May your hooks stay busy, your yarn stay colorful, and your creations continue to bring smiles and warmth to the world.

Happy crocheting!
With warm regards,
Sonia Kenzie

Addendum 1: Doll Charts and Special Holiday Pattern

Unlock a Special Holiday Pattern Just for You and Enhance Your Crochet Experience with Downloadable Charts!

1. Simplify your crochet projects with easily accessible charts for every pattern in this book.
2. Enjoy a more visual and efficient crochet experience for all your projects.
3. Join our crochet community for more tips, FREE PATTERNS, and exclusive content for special occasions!

Scan the QR Code below to Access and Download All FREE CONTENT Featured in This Book:

Made in the USA
Las Vegas, NV
16 April 2024